STRIPPED DOWN:

How Burlesque Led Me Home

By Anna Brooke, aka Rev. Legs Malone

Stripped Down: How Burlesque Led Me Home

ISBN: 978-1-733419-76-5

Library of Congress Control Number: 2020902583

Cover Design: Meredith Hancock, hancockmedia.com

Cover Photo: Leland Bobbé

Interior Layout & Formatting: Ronda Taylor, heartworkpublishing.com

The Unapologetic Voice House
Scottsdale, AZ
www.theunapologeticvoicehouse.com

Dedicated to all my teachers. Thank you for generously sharing your wisdom that has deeply and lovingly impacted my life so that I may help enrich the lives of others.

Contents

Foreword

As you read Legs Malone's book, I hope you experience some of the excitement I've enjoyed in burlesque. The feeling of accepting glamour as a form of resistance (as Mx Justin Vivian Bond recommends). The feeling of allowing myself to see and love the audience, allowing the audience to see and love me, have transformed the way I think about being in my body and spirit. When I teach burlesque, it is always heartening to watch a roomful of people look into the mirror during classes and see them smile as they react to themselves. When those who choose to take it to the stage step into the light, it all becomes magnified. The audience receives and throws that self-love right back to them.

The longer I teach, the more I learn from my students. They teach me how to communicate by responding when I succeed in it; they teach me how to be compassionate by responding with enthusiasm when I'm attentive to their journeys; and ultimately, they teach me how to teach by showing me which parts of my teaching work and which don't.

Legs Malone did all of this, but she also taught me how to view myself as something more than a machine who does the job.

I had been performing and teaching for so long that, although I hadn't entirely lost my joy, I was drowning in pragmatism. I knew what happened when I did a particular thing. I knew how to lead an audience, whether at a show or in a classroom, and I knew where they wanted to go. What I had all but forgotten was what my journey meant to me.

I get caught up in the idea of service to my audience, my students, and my community as a form of duty, but the reality is that there is no giving without give and take. Legs gently reminded me of this as she shared her story. She talked about more than getting the gig and making the audience happy. She talked about the emotional and spiritual journey of discovering how to share herself with them.

Because my early approach to burlesque was so punk rock in so many ways, so committed to individuality and so repulsed by conformity, I didn't want to think about spiritual woo-woo or goddesses or mindfulness. But Legs, without even deliberately intending to, led me to see that all those things supported my individuality while helping me be of more service to my students. She led by example, keeping her sharp sense of humor even as she maintained her kindness and sensitivity.

Her belief in burlesque as spiritual endeavor and her description of it as a healing practice, which had seemed to me at first to be destined to be disillusioned, worked for her. As I watched it work for her it began to work for me, too.

I'm still a pragmatist and a technician, a teacher who knows exactly how things work and why. I know how to find the light and what filter to put on it. However, thanks to Legs, I also know that the spotlight is not just about grabbing it, not just about accepting myself as someone who looks the way I look in it, and not just about telling my story, but about reflecting that light back to others, and giving them a chance to shine.

I've watched Legs step into the spotlight of the teacher. It is a pleasure to have a former student become an instructor and know that this practice of healing through performance, seduction, glamour, and self-love is being made available in new ways.

I encourage all readers to consider trying burlesque for themselves. Go go to a show, to begin with. Become a student, whether formally or informally. As an audience member, student, or instructor, keep that light shining bright.

Jo Weldon
Headmistress of The New York School of Burlesque and author of *The Burlesque Handbook*

Introduction: Why This and Why Me?

Who am I?

This question is one that people have asked themselves for millennia. Countless storytellers and philosophers continue to ponder and explore this age-old need for certainty. This yearning for knowledge has birthed multitudes of religions and dogmas, not to mention countless writings, scientific explorations and artistic endeavors that attempt to answer this query.

This question also is deeply personal and connects us all in a singular quest for meaning.

For me, it showed itself in a journal entry from my anguished early 20s. "Who would I be if I stopped smoking cigarettes and drinking coffee? Will people still like me? Will we have anything to talk about?"

I look back at that time, thankfully, now, with a lot of love in my heart and a much deeper sense of compassion for myself. But I still remember the all-consuming pain, despair and an almost total lack of sense of self that defined my days. These deeper questions of identity and belonging took root early and continued to grow throughout my 20s and 30s. The absence of a satisfying answer to that seminal question above made me feel helpless and lost. There was nothing I could turn to that could assist me in these confused moments. There was no pill I could take or item of clothing I could buy that would quiet the feelings of uncertainty and deep unease.

What I did know was that I loved dancing and art. Put on a good song and I wouldn't have a snowball's chance in hell of staying still.

When I was old enough, I loved going out and dancing the night away. Everything else—school, work, commitments—felt impossible and doomed to failure. I was willing to do whatever was asked or needed of me in order to feel like I mattered, and yet I would drag my feet on anything I didn't like, which got me in plenty of hot water with my parents, teachers, and friends. I felt adrift, endlessly treading water in an ocean of indifference and zero motivation. The shoreline was nowhere in sight and I seemed to be content with this state of passive limbo.

The truth was this: I had no idea who I was. I felt like I was water, taking the shape of whatever container I was currently poured into. I remember repeatedly coming up against this urgent question of identity and belonging, frantically asking and needing an answer as I felt my life and its circumstances change around me. During one particularly fraught and vulnerable moment, one of my mentors very calmly and lovingly told me that my essence would never change no matter how much changed on the outside. That rocked me. What did she mean? Did she mean that no matter what I did, I would always be the same? Did I even like what was at my core? Who the hell would I be if I peeled away all my masks? If I shed all my protective behaviors? It boiled down to that same, crucial question, who was I beneath all the layers of meaning I had heaped upon myself? I was desperate to know.

As a healer now I see so many people deeply attached to external factors as a gauge of their personal value. From education to jobs to what brand of shoes or clothes one wears, people attach meaning and validation to a vast array of *things*. The same goes for physical appearances obviously.

But why do we believe that if we become more attractive on the outside that we are somehow more desirable or lovable? Does that have any bearing on our worthiness and our value? (Spoiler alert: The answer is no). Are we somehow unloveable if we gain weight, or go through a change that impacts our appearance? Are we only our bodies and nothing more? (Also no.) What kind of physical, emotional or spiritual toll does this way of thinking take on our body? (Answer: a big one) How do we free ourselves of this so we can live our lives?

Questions like this contributed ruinously to my constant state of fear and anxiety. I found that I could manage these uncomfortable emotions by controlling and limiting what I ate. My feelings of unworthiness became a marathon of deprivation and I was committed to believing I was not enough. This manifested as anorexia during my high school and college years. This swiftly adapted disorder gave me a sense of control in my very out-of-control life. My starvation started as a diet regime, a sort of destructive hobby that ended up taking over and dominating my life. I remember looking at myself in a mirror when I was at my most unwell, knowing what I was doing to my body was destructive. But still I felt a perverse sense of satisfaction and accomplishment at the same time. My eating disorder gave me control and a sense of purpose. To become a size 2 at 5'11" was an achievement beyond measure. I thought that if I could control what was coming into my body and what I was receiving as nourishment, that I could control everything in my life too.

Sweet, loveable me, I had no idea how sick I really was. I remember spending hours looking at my reflection in the mirror. It was as if I was tethered to my own likeness by an invisible unyielding rope. I held myself to impossible and toxic physical beauty standards. I would obsess over my need to wear the right clothes, to ace all the other external qualities I believed made me more desirable or attractive in the eyes of others. Deep down I knew there was something more to all of this. And yet I drove my body and my health into the ground with unrelenting dedication.

Looking back, I realize that my disorder materialized from the fact that I had abstained from taking charge of my life. I consistently assigned control to something outside of myself. I wanted to avoid responsibility and engagement in my own life because both of those things felt really scary. For a very long time, I never questioned this behavior despite being really tired of never having/being/doing enough as a result.

Here's the thing: when we give our power to something outside of ourselves, we rescind our innate ability to make choices and commitments that resonate with our own hearts. When we create a codependent identity with things, relationships or events that have happened in our lives, we discount our own agency and inhibit our ability to create new visions, possibilities, and action plans. We are vibrant co-creators with the Divine, and when we say no to that truth, we are saying no to our birthright of abundance, belonging and love.

MY BIRTH INTO BURLESQUE

In 2006, I was in a real pickle. I was living in London, a dearly held dream of mine. I had just completed my Master's Degree in Contemporary Art. Studying art history was the only thing that academically ever made sense to me. I had serendipitously scored a great internship at an arts organization that was run on heart, passion and a very tight budget. It didn't matter the hours of labor—I felt like I was making a difference and was right in the thick of a super exciting moment in contemporary art history in one of the coolest cities in the world.

When my student visa expired in late January of 2006, I immediately started trying to figure out how I could stay. For me, returning to the U.S. felt non-negotiable. It would have meant that I had failed, and that was unacceptable. I had left behind a lot of pain and heartbreak in New York that made it too uncomfortable to think about returning.

I also loved my job and the identity it provided, not to mention my access to the glamorous art world. I was living my dream and I was incredibly happy. My reverie was dented only by one thing: having to hide. I was technically an illegal immigrant and was not allowed to be seen working for the organization in any way, shape or form. This meant I was not allowed to be seen working or get paid for my work. As you might imagine, this did a real number on me. Over many months, the forced hiding and skirting of the law slowly ate away at me. I was working towards the greater goal of staying in the U.K. and establishing a new life. But deep down, I was unsettled and knew something had to change.

My job submitted a work visa sponsorship application and the prospects looked promising. I started to weave a rather complicated narrative for immigration officials so I could stay as long as possible and safely under the radar on a six-month tourist visa. I went home to the U.S. upon expiry of my student visa only to return to the U.K. two weeks later under the guise of surprising a non-existent boyfriend for Valentine's Day. I stayed there for another few weeks and then returned home to the U.S. for five weeks. I wasn't allowed to work at my job while on British soil, but I could from my native land, so home I went.

Therein started a slow, excruciating process of transition and transformation that would be studded with unexpected twists that forever changed the course of my life.

Upon landing at my mother's home in the Berkshires of Western Massachusetts at the start of a five-week trip, I was able to stop and breathe. Working like crazy had distracted me from what was really going on. I came face-to-face with the fact that I was not well. Physically, I was fine, but my nervous system was shot and emotionally I was a mess. Due to the consistent stress of my visa and work situation, I had lost track of me. I had forgotten what I wanted and had no idea what I even needed. I had become so accustomed to fulfilling the needs of others that my needs weren't even a consideration. My proverbial tanks were empty and I felt lost and hopeless.

While sitting on my mom's couch trying to catch my emotional breath, I opened up a brochure to one of my favorite centers of healing and wellness. While I was struggling for insight and direction a few years earlier, I had attended massage school there and this place held a very special place in my heart. While there, my old, painful wounds were revealed to me in the safety of love and profound grace. I gained tools and information that fortified me with both experience and strength so I could bring healing work to others as I embarked on my own healing journey. This place was a safe, home base where I could get back to what really mattered to me.

I opened up the brochure and looked at what was offered during my week-long stay. My eyes were drawn to a workshop titled "Trust Your Vibes," led by a world-renowned intuitive. It wasn't what I initially had in mind, but it had to do with listening to your sixth sense and trusting your own intuition, something I felt I was sorely lacking. I registered, and a few days later, off I went.

The workshop was held in the great hall of the retreat center. I remember walking in and feeling thrilled by the cathedral-like atmosphere. I was overcome with gratitude at the chance to hit the pause button on my chaotic, disorganized and uncertain life. I was a mix of emotions fueled by nostalgic memories of my former experiences there and excited anticipation for the weekend ahead.

An integral part of the workshop was dancing, one of my favorite activities in the world. The instructor constantly asked us to move our bodies and dance in order to free up any inner energies and beliefs that were holding us back. At one point, I remember dancing as a group. The leader yelled out, "loosen up!" I guess we looked pretty stiff, even though I thought I was moving pretty fluidly and freely.

As this command hit me, I was suddenly, keenly aware of how much I was holding back.

Since early childhood, I wanted to burst onto the stage to share my light and my love. But fear of the judgment of others created a mesh of resistance through which I could not pass. In my life, I felt happy and vibrant at times, but only under certain conditions. When the workshop leader commanded us to just let go and dance again, I leaped into the aisle in full view of everyone and danced my ass off with wild abandon. I felt completely exposed and totally liberated. In that split second, I chose to say yes and jumped into the small spotlight in this one room. At that moment, I understood the saying: one small step for man, one giant leap for mankind. I was amazed at how expansive it felt. I remember thinking, (despite insecurities biting at my ankles), "I belong here."

During the last session of the weekend, we sat for a guided meditation. The workshop facilitator instructed us to relax our whole body and receive messages from our intuition. She began by telling us to ask our sixth sense where our greatest joy lay in our lives. She encouraged us to really listen to the answers. When her gentle prompting came to the topic of work and career, she told us to ask ourselves: "what would bring me the greatest joy for work?"

Immediately, as if someone's lips were up against my right ear, I heard the words "burlesque dancer."

It felt like a bolt of lightning in my body.

I opened my eyes and quickly looked to the right where the voice had come from. The only person there was about five feet away, fully absorbed in her own meditation. My arm hairs were standing on end and it felt as if pure electricity was coursing through my body. Not only did the thought of being a dancer as a job thrill and confound me, but I also had no idea what being a burlesque dancer actually meant. Clearly, it involved dance, but what on earth was burlesque?

When the meditation was complete, we paired up to share our experiences with each other. I told my partner what I had received and her jaw dropped. All she said was "WOW." Seeing her response was both exciting and super confusing. I still felt the resonance of the electricity running through my body but my mind was whirling. I had just been told by a disembodied voice to do something that I had no idea about what it actually was, and my body was vibrating in response. I couldn't ignore the strong signals I was getting, but I couldn't make any sense of them either.

When I got home that afternoon, I ran to my mom's computer and immediately googled 'burlesque dancer.' When the definition and images popped up on my screen, I was stunned. Gorgeous women of all shapes and sizes in various states of undress filled the screen. I saw a picture of the "Original Bazoom Girl" Jennie

Lee twirling tassels. My jaw dropped. Some spirit or ghost or my own imagination had just guided me to this art form that involved both performance AND striptease?! I remember sitting back in the chair, practically in shock at this alien concept that had clearly landed so firmly in my body.

Amid my shock and awe, my next step was to search for classes. If this was to be my joyful job, I wanted to get started learning about it. I was heading down to NYC for a month to stay with friends, and promptly found the New York School of Burlesque. I signed up for the next available class which was fan dancing. I roped my best friend into it, and on one sultry NYC spring day, we showed up in a dance studio in Astor Place. The headmistress herself, Jo Boobs, taught the class.

I will never forget holding two small feather fans in various poses and catching a glimpse of myself in the mirror. After years of trying to be someone I wasn't and hating myself, my body suddenly made sense to me. Its length, shape, and lines aligned so beautifully with these playful, little props. It took my breath away. For the first time in my life, I both looked and felt beautiful, and I was amazed.

I continued to take burlesque classes and developed a voracious appetite for all things burlesque. I dove into YouTube videos, books, articles, blogs, whatever I could get my hands and eyes on, and consumed it hungrily.

Soon thereafter, I received my first of three work visa rejections. As my U.K. work visa and residency hopes ultimately began to fade, burlesque became my oasis and my salvation. I was going back and forth between London and New York trying to maintain some semblance of normalcy amid the crumbling of my dreams. I continued to take classes while working undercover for my job. I even started to choreograph my first burlesque routine in my London bedroom, after my roommates had gone to sleep. Dancing around and working out choreography felt so good. Night after night, I kept playing with it. As I became more hopeless and despondent about being able to stay in the U.K., burlesque was a beacon that brought me fulfillment and joy.

On the morning of September 6, 2006, I started my day, as was my habit, by reading my horoscope. It was a new moon that day, a very auspicious time for new beginnings, and my horoscope told me that whatever seeds I planted on that day could grow larger than I ever imagined. I was registered for a burlesque class that night with the legendary Jo King at The Bethnal Green Working Men's Club in London - that was to be followed by an amateur show. I had made a great friend, Torie, at an earlier class, and we had become fellow enthusiasts of all things burlesque. Torie and I had both signed up for the class and intended to watch the amateur show afterward from the safety of our seats.

The class was magnificent and as we settled in for the show to follow, I noticed a woman walking around to every table and asking questions to subsequently shaking heads. When she got to our table she told us that most of the performers for the amateur show had dropped out and they were down to only two performers. They desperately needed people to step forward to make the show happen, and asked us if we would like to perform. Torie, a proper English woman, immediately shook her head and said no. I too said no, but was stunned that there was an opportunity to get on stage that night. Torie must have noticed the look on my face, and she asked me if I actually wanted to get up there. With my morning's horoscope swirling around in my head and a swelling feeling of possibility in my gut, I sheepishly said yes, but that I needed some props to actually make it happen. When I shared with Torie what they were (a trenchcoat and pasties along with a couple of other props), she bent over her overstuffed bag and pulled out a beige trench and white-and-black swirl pasties. The other props were easily attained at the bar. I knew then and there that I was getting up on that stage come hell or high water. When the show producer came back around looking for performers I volunteered much to her delight. She asked my stage name, and for the first time out loud, I said: "Legs Malone."

I remember huddling behind the monitor that acted as the wings for the stage. I was trembling. My heart was racing. My palms turned more sweaty and cold with each passing second. I thought to myself, "it's now or never," and when my brand new moniker was announced, I stepped on stage for the very first time, racing heart and all.

I would love to say that my first time on stage was an unequivocal success, but in reality, the performance was a total disaster. I stopped listening to the music once I saw the audience in front of me. I bumbled through what I was supposed to do, only to realize the song was ending and I still needed to strip down. I sped through a hasty clothing drop with fumbled props followed by a tepid tassel twirl, and I was done.

There were three judges, two of whom were lovely and really supportive and one who was rather harsh in her assessment of my maiden voyage in striptease. Despite feeling a little hurt by the third judge's opinion, I felt as if a light had just been lit in the core of my being. The producer and judges all came up to me afterward and congratulated me for my bravery in getting up there with little to no notice for my very first time. They told me that I should return the next month to compete again. These amateur nights were going to happen each month, and the winners of each would come back for a grand finale and competition at the end of the year. I thanked them, still quivering from the adrenaline, and made note of every single future date.

As I walked Torie to the train afterward, I could hardly speak. I don't even know if I could blink. I got home and tried to go to bed, but I couldn't sleep. I stared at the ceiling for hours. Part of me knew that I had just started the next chapter of my life and the rest of me couldn't make sense of what was happening. All I knew was that I was alight in every cell of my body, and there was no turning back.

I competed in the next month's amateur night with an act as an ode to my immigration plight. I danced behind two British flags to "You'll Lose a Good Thing" by Carla Thomas, from the classic Hairspray movie soundtrack. I won the competition that night, securing my spot in the final. My win was a considerable bright spot as I had just gotten a second rejection for my work visa, further dimming my hopes of British residency.

The timing of everything felt like a giant cosmic joke. Within a few weeks, my job's big event was happening and I wasn't allowed to be named, seen, or acknowledged. I was exhausted, heartsick and broke. I bought a one-way ticket to return to New York once everything with work was wrapped up. I couldn't keep holding on anymore. Instead of holding on to what felt like a fraying rope, I decided to go home, come what may, and await the final decision. I booked my ticket home for the day after the final burlesque competition so at least I could compete before returning to the states.

To my utter and bittersweet delight, I won the final burlesque competition on the same stage on which I was so nervously born upon a few months prior. Not only was it a massive thrill, but I also won a nice cash prize to boot. I stayed up all night partying and celebrating with my ebullient friends. At the same time, I was mourning my departure with many bottles of champagne and too many shots to count. I blurrily got home as the sun was rising, grabbed my bags and headed to the airport. I used my winnings to buy myself very expensive sunglasses while I was waiting for my flight. I had a wicked hangover and my eyes were puffy from crying, but I also knew that this newly minted star needed fancy glasses to navigate the crowds, photo ops and the challenges of being a famous person in public. After all, I had just won the first-ever amateur burlesque competition in all of London and that in itself was a pipe dream come true. Anna Brooke was heading home in abject failure and suffocating grief, but as I walked on to that plane I knew Legs Malone's star had been born. There was no looking back.

I never got my work visa, and I had to make the heartbreaking decision to leave my life in the U.K. and permanently move back to the U.S. I flew back to London, packed up my room, tied up all my loose ends, and said my goodbyes. The sadness of that time was punctuated by my biggest burlesque booking yet where I got to be the star of the closing act of a rather posh event. The doldrums of my imminent departure were set in sharp contrast by the success of my new persona, the rising star that was Legs Malone. That celebration and visibility gave me a lot of comfort and hope as I unwillingly moved back to New York for good.

Once there, I cried for two months. I left everything I was in the U.K. I had no job, no prestige, and no discernible community. I was living at my dad and stepmom's apartment in New York, barely able to get out of bed and face the reality of my life. Burlesque remained my saving grace, and every night for weeks on end, I went to every single burlesque show I could find in New York. It took me weeks to even let my friends know I was home. The disappointment and feelings of failure were more than I could handle. But night after night, from the dark anonymous safety of the audience, I drank up the spectacle of sequins, dancing girls, scripted and unscripted shows, and countless twirling pasties. I knew that one day if I was lucky and worked really hard, I would be up on those stages with those amazing artists.

As I reflect on that time, I realize that I had been stripped down in more ways than one. The concept of my identity had been challenged to the core and I felt totally hopeless. Little did I know that burlesque would be a bright beacon that would lead me back home to my heart. As I surrendered to my new reality, I slowly started to pick up gigs. My persistent attendance led to lots of introductions and performances in some great shows. Before I knew it, I was performing weekly, and then three times a week and then so frequently that it became my full-time job.

I look back on that time with a mixture of gratitude and disbelief. How the hell did I leave a promising career in the arts to become a full-time striptease artist? I had two degrees that quickly began to gather dust as I learned how to hone my art, how to do my hair and when and where to *not* use glitter.

Before long, I booked my first West Coast tour, and then my second. I performed at the Edinburgh Fringe Festival two summers in a row. I performed in Stockholm as a headliner. I had beautiful homecomings on stages throughout England. Before long, I was gigging full time in New York City with as many as nine shows in a week. Within a few years, I had become a full-time dancer pounding the city's pavement and go-go boxes between bars, clubs, restaurants, and theaters. I didn't know where all of this was going to lead, but what I did know is that I was happier than I had ever been. At long last, I had found my tribe, and I had found myself. Love, fulfillment and a deep sense of belonging greeted me in the most unexpected places, all because I listened to my heart and a disembodied voice that came from a higher power who had my highest good in mind. Amid the crumbling structures of my life, the echo of that voice in my heart led me to a most unexpected and deeply fulfilling place that opened up the rest of my life.

A back injury ended my burlesque career as I knew it in early 2016. I went from dancing nightly to being laid up on the couch unable to move. It was a very quiet and sad time for me, and it forced me to begin thinking about life offstage. Clearly, I wasn't going to be able to dance for a living forever, but everything came screeching to a halt much earlier than I anticipated. After a long time of mourning and negotiation of new ways to move and treat my body, I had a flash one day that reset me. I saw myself driving down a highway and instead of looking ahead toward where I was going, I was turned around, watching what I was leaving get smaller and farther away behind me. I was so consumed with what I was leaving that I hadn't thought to turn around and look where I was headed. That realization lifted a weight I hadn't known I was carrying. I realized that just because my life as I had known it was ending did not mean my life was over. I am typing these words more than three years later as an interdisciplinary healing arts practitioner and teacher who still gets on stage, just wearing more sensible heels.

Life didn't end, it just changed.

Burlesque brought me up against many truths of freedom, of agency and of the practice of unconditional love for my community, and myself. What I was thoroughly unprepared for was how it brought me home to love. Burlesque provided me with the conditions to bring the forces of Divinity and love into the core of my being. My burlesque family showed me that my beliefs around power, limitations, and judgment were untrue. I was brought to my knees on more than one occasion as I realized how limited and self-negating many of my beliefs were. I am so grateful for the fearless love that this form and my community showed me.

To that Original, Sacred voice, I bow and offer my deep thanks.

To myself, I offer gratitude and acknowledgment for saying yes, taking this crazy chance and for reading my horoscope that morning all those years ago.

To you, dear reader, I say thank you for buying and reading this book. This book charts the crucial lessons I had to learn over the course of my own negotiations and navigations so that I could land more fully in the vibration of love. I acknowledge the part of you that sees a reflection of yourself in these words. I also offer some practical exercises that will help you hear the guiding voice inside yourself. I hope you will take heart from my story and know that if you are burdened by false or limiting ideas, you are not alone. And those ideas don't have to stay

I salute the part of you that wants to be expressed in benevolence and pure joy, the aspects of your spirit that want to come out and be heard and celebrated. I turn up the volume for the part of you who is ready to dance your soul and its purpose with wild abandon. The world is ready and hungry for you to show up with your gifts and offer them so you, and we, can all lead richer, more fulfilling lives.

Thank you for reading. Thank you for being a part of my journey. May you always know the light of your own love. I hope you enjoy what I have written.

ONE

Burlesque the Beginning: The Celebration of the Sensual, Sacred Feminine

If you've never been to a burlesque show, I encourage you to put this book down, find the closest show, and book tickets now. I'll be here waiting when you get back to reading.

Burlesque shows are fun, sexy and playful spectacles that involve the reveal of the unclothed human form through the art of striptease. These shows are joy incarnate, especially when they are performed with heart, soul and a desire to celebrate the human form in its sparkly, practically nude glory.

Burlesque is the art of the striptease whose primary medium is the body. Performed predominantly by (but not limited to) women, this style of dance is revolutionary, feminist and unapologetic. It can be humorous, horrifying, gorgeous and anything else it wants to be, but above all it is creative! I personally feel that burlesque is the inheritance and expression of sacred, sensual female power. Harnessing it is a gift that can change you forever.

The word "burlesque" comes from the Italian word *burlesco*, from the root *burla* meaning "mockery." Popularized in the Commedia dell'Arte, the term "burlesque" was widely used to indicate a grotesque or over-exaggerated mockery by a character or actor on stage. This term came to be common as an indicator of parody across different artistic disciplines.

Just as painters use paint and canvas and sculptors clay or bronze, burlesque as an art form uses the medium of the body. No matter the appearance of the body, burlesque shows us that we can create a revolution of perception by simply showing up and being seen while we do what we love the most.

I find burlesque shows to be bastions of artistic and creative freedom that provide delightful respite from the real world outside the venue doors. When I was first attending shows in New York City as a way to escape the despair of my post-London life, I felt I was witnessing the intersection of time and space studded with rhinestones in surprising places.

If you are in or near a big city, you may more easily find burlesque shows, but they also exist in smaller towns. Go support them. They are holding down a crucial corner of the universe and you may find you've changed for the better as a result of attending.

As an art form, burlesque can be titillating, inspiring, sensual, erotic, and deeply pleasurable. For some people, it also can be an uncomfortable and triggering experience. I have witnessed many responses and reactions to burlesque acts, from flushed, excited hollering to cold indifference. Leave it to an unclothed, sensual body expressing itself live and in-person to bring up all sorts of feelings, responses, and reactions.

As burlesque dancers, our bodies are both our canvas and our toolbox. Our art cannot be separated from our bodies. Some criticisms can get very tangled up between the art, the medium and the artist, which are not one and the same for other art forms.

When I started doing burlesque, it became my life. I remember being backstage, surrounded by the naked bodies of my fellow performers in various states of preparation for their act, and thinking about what a massive blessing it all was. Being welcomed into a world where people were seen because they chose to do so was immensely rewarding for me. I had never seen women *own* their bodies the way my new friends and colleagues did. These women were inhabiting their bodies with power and joy while dancing and speaking truth to THEIR art and no one else's. The performers were consciously saying yes to the part of them that felt deep joy in the act of creation and self-expression. I was consistently inspired and moved by what these women brought onto the stage.

Backstage alongside me were women who worked corporate day jobs, moms whose partners or friends were home watching the kids, and fellow artists stringing together gigs to make enough money so they could continue making their art. Among this amazing group of people, there was solidarity and a kind of kinship I had never known before. We looked out for each other. We gave warm words of encouragement as well as honest feedback. An overall sense of tribe and community permeated my experience getting into burlesque. I found sisterhood, family, love and a multiplicity of hilarious, warm, beloved relationships with wonderful, wacky people with whom I am beyond fortunate to share a deep soul connection.

When I am on stage, I am in heaven. There is an intoxicating electricity at the moment when my choreographed moves elicit whistles and whoops. I get to play with a whole group of people whose sole job it is to watch me and my art for their enjoyment. I realize this might sound like a kind of hell for some, but for me it was bliss.

Burlesque was never a choice for me, but an assignment that came directly from the center of my heart. As I began to rehearse new acts, the only hurdle I faced was navigating and negotiating my own self-hate and criticism. The flood of joy that lit me up washed away any semblance of prior hesitation or resistance. I can't compare the feeling to anything else. It was as if a torrential flood of light was unleashed in me and spilled out in every direction. How on earth could I ever say no to that?

It is essential when talking about burlesque to honor its history. We owe huge gratitude to the many women who were willing to dismantle the mores of polite society in order to electrify audiences.

There are male, drag and trans performers as well whose contributions are crucially important. They are often not as well known as famed burlesque women, but their work is part of the legacy that we all inhabit.

Our foremothers of burlesque planted the seeds for the global burlesque community of today whose numbers are exponentially growing. These descriptions hardly contain the multitudes of achievement by these women. I encourage you to use this as a launching off point to dive into the rich herstory of burlesque.

Lydia Thompson

In 1868, a British woman named Lydia Thompson brought her all-female dance troupe, The British Blondes, to New York City. These women rocked New York by performing in knee-length skirts while wearing thick, white woolen tights. Her famous show *Ixion* featured women playing every role, a novelty for the time that thoroughly roiled the prim and proper. Coming out of Victorian Britain, Lydia was well-versed in how to put on a great show. She had started performing at age 15 in pantomimes in Britain and had slowly built up her expertise and reputation over many years. Lydia and her gender-bending, boundary-pushing early feminism made a massive splash in the U.S. She was an early, unapologetic feminist whose art and work was the beginning of a tsunami of sensual, performative art in American social history.

Little Egypt

The originator of the "hootchie kootch" dance, Little Egypt danced the 1893 Chicago World's Fair into a frenzy. Her bumping, grinding style of belly dancing was so risqué that very little video footage remains of her. The few clips that remain have a railroad-track style filter over her breasts and hips to block out her gyrating movements. Her famous style of bellydance gave way to the infamous bump and grind that became a staple of burlesque movement.

Sally Rand

One of the earliest and most famous fan dancers, Sally Rand's enormous ostrich feather fans and her skill in using them made her a legend. She was an innovator in the use of fans to hide her often completely naked body. This led the way for feather fans to become a signature prop and tool for burlesque acts. She is also credited to have invented the bubble dance, which involved her dancing with a giant balloon on stage. She too rocked the Chicago World's Fair in 1933, allegedly getting arrested four times in one day for indecency during her acts.

Gypsy Rose Lee

Gypsy Rose Lee is one of the most famous burlesque dancers in history. In addition to her long career on stage, she was also a writer whose life story was portrayed in the film *Gypsy* starring Natalie Wood. Her famous banter and quick wit were paired with a mastery of the 'tease' in striptease. She kept performing until she was 45 years old but later said that "a woman over 30 should keep on her clothes.... I was asked why I still took mine off and I replied, 'Just to prove my point.'"

Jennie Lee

Known as "The Bazoom Girl", Jennie Lee was the founder of Exotic World, a burlesque museum that is now the Burlesque Hall of Fame. She was a union organizer and an activist for the rights of strippers and sex workers. In 1955, she created the first union for dancers, Exotic Dancers' League of North America and was its first president. Born to protect the rights of exotic dancers, EDL helped fight for better pay and fair treatment of the girls whose living and working conditions were neither regulated nor protected. Lee was a trailblazer who set the tone for feminist activism in a time when it was practically unheard of. The EDL slowly morphed into a social organization and a place for retired dancers to gather and reminisce. Old costume pieces of fellow dancers, including many g-strings, started to accumulate on the walls of the bar that Lee and her husband owned. Before long, Lee founded Exotic World, a museum of burlesque and its many artifacts, transforming an old goat farm in the desert of Helendale, California. Lee turned Exotic World over to another former dancer and dear friend, Dixie Evans. She died in 1990.

Dixie Evans

Evans was known as the Marilyn Monroe of Burlesque. Born in the 1920s in Georgia, Evans was a well-known star on the burlesque circuit. She was famous for her bawdy and delightfully raunchy acts, some of which can be seen on YouTube. After Jennie Lee's death, Evans single-handedly manned and maintained Exotic World and its extensive collection. Once visitors passed beneath a huge sign that said EXOTIC WORLD, they would see a hand-painted sign hung outside the museum that instructed visitors to honk a number of times for a tour. No matter what time of day it was, Dixie would come out and personally give a tour of the collection to whoever had made the pilgrimage to the rickety building that housed these priceless relics. Evans maintained the collection until its move to Vegas in 2007. Evans passed away in 2013 but her legacy lives on in the museum and in the hearts of those who were fortunate enough to know and love her. I never got to visit Helendale but I am so grateful for the efforts of these amazing women so that we can reap the bounty of their richly lived and danced lives.

To name each and every legend of burlesque falls outside of the scope of this book. However, I will happily plant the seeds of curiosity for you to dive deeper into this incredible history. Know and research the following names (listed in no particular order) and know that there are countless more waiting in the wings. You won't be sorry.

Lili St. Cyr, Tempest Storm, April March, Rose La Rose, Toni Elling, Lottie the Body, Lily Christine, Wild Cherry, Candy Barr, Honi Harlow, Kitten Natividad, Camille 2000, Viva La Fever, Judith Stein, Dusty Summers, Satan's Angel, Tura Satana, Sherry Britton, Blaze Starr, Alexandra the Great 48, Velvet Ice, Ellion Ness, Candy

Caramelo, Holiday O'Hara, Tura Satana, Wah Wah Taysee (Taysie), Noel Toy, Jadin Wong, Barbara Yung, and countless more.

The contemporary burlesque performers I admire and love could themselves fill up an entire book on their own. In lieu of listing them here, I have dedicated each chapter of this book to fellow performers whose work has greatly impacted me.

BURLESQUE AS ACTIVISM AND AGENCY

"In some ways, it's the job of a woman to be looked at in our culture. When you get onstage and you show your body and you make a decision through your art about how you want people to see you, you're actually becoming an agent in negotiating the way you are looked at. And that's very powerful for a lot of women."

—Jezebel Express, neo-burlesque performer and teacher

There is an archetype of the sacred sensual woman that has been simultaneously worshipped and reviled for millennia. Inanna, Ishtar, Mohini, and Mary Magdalene are some of the examples of this untamed, unapologetic archetype. I define this particular sensual, female archetype as a woman who has free agency to use her body and mind to do her work. This archetype encompasses the ancient temple dancers, sacred sexual healers, and more recently witches, strippers, and sex workers. Society generally does not accept this kind of woman. She is highlighted in the classic Madonna/Whore complex and has been pigeonholed as a tramp and a threat to established society. If men are tempted away from their wives and families, it is frequently purported to be the other woman's fault, not the man's. Somehow for a woman to claim and own her own sensuality is to threaten the very fabric of society. Why? It boils down to the fact that men cannot own or control these women and either can't or don't want to control themselves in the face of such unapologetic beauty.

Religions and governments alike have come down hard on women throughout the ages. The cumulative blows on female freedom of expression have been ruinous for women and anyone who bears predominant female energy or appearance. The subsequent commodification of female sexuality and sensuality by the powers that be has created a complicated paradigm for anyone who wants to access that original and sacred energy inherent in all our bodies and souls. Too many women have been forced into sex work out of deprivation or worse, sexual slavery. This extreme and yet nauseatingly common example encompasses a much darker shadow side to our world. A pervasive part of our culture throughout time is deeply invested in the suppression, oppression, and commodification of the sacred, sensual female body. The breadcrumb trail leads back to a deep patriarchal fear of empowered women. It is past time we give her back her autonomy and strength so we can find a new level of balance and strength in our world.

This is why burlesque matters so much to me. It represents a reclamation of our inherent, sensual freedom and the agency so long denied to us. Burlesque is a grand, glorious middle finger to patriarchal society and all its institutions. It is a revelatory celebration of the body as art. Whether an act is hilariously funny or heart-stoppingly beautiful, the dancers who offer themselves body, heart and mind are functioning in service of a much higher, divine truth (whether they know it or not).

When I say that burlesque is love, I mean it.

For a woman to tap into her own agency, her own ability to connect and make things happen on her own terms is a powerful thing. In burlesque, the performer calls all the shots on how they choose to move, dress and express, with zero unsolicited input from anyone outside. In what other industry or art form can women be in charge of all aspects of their work? Where else can the feminine form and energy be celebrated while empowering both the artist and the audience? I don't know of any other field where a woman so thoroughly can be in charge of the concept, construction, and delivery of her work. This is doubly the case with burlesque because this has been the precedent for decades.

Even in the golden age of burlesque of the 1940s–1950s, when men were predominantly running the shows and booking the girls, the women themselves had a unique outlet for their own creativity. Nowadays, there are majority female-run shows in the burlesque world. I have been fortunate to produce and perform in many female-run shows over the years.

Our world needs a grand reintroduction and re-indoctrination into the innocence of the female form and its inherent beauty and worth. We are living in a time when duality is more dominant than ever. We are told to believe someone is always better/prettier/stronger/more valuable than someone else. This duality serves no other purpose than to separate us from one another. This binary opposition is sinking our ship faster than we can bail it out.

How long have women been limited in their own physical expression? How long has the female body been oppressed and loaded with concepts of commodification, sin, otherness, and dirtiness? How many major religions have written into their holy texts that women are to be submissive to their husbands and fathers? How many millions of baby girls have been killed because their lives were seen as worthless? We see a multitude of examples that this diseased perspective of duality is alive and well. But, if we wish to see lasting change, we cannot end this mentality by attacking it with rage and vitriol. Those same emotions are what put those beliefs into motion in the first place. To paraphrase Einstein, we cannot solve the problem with the same mindset that created it.

In order for us to come back into connection with our original inherent equality and with one another, we must look within. We must weed out any belief that says women are "less than" and thus second or even third-class citizens whose treatment does not matter because their lives simply don't matter as much as men's do. It is time for us to acknowledge that women and female bodies are worthy of unconditional love and loving treatment. We need to recognize that when a woman is in charge of her body, we all benefit. We can free up the locked corners of our own minds when we watch a woman dance. We can allow ourselves to delight in her passion and free self-expression, knowing that we are witnessing spirit in motion. We can begin to understand that when we give ourselves permission to find meaning, value, and purpose in what brings us joy, we can easily bask in the light of a woman and the radiant beauty that emanates from her. There is no threat in a woman in charge of her own body and life choices, no matter how many terrified men in power say otherwise. To be a woman is a gift. It's time we start walking with this concept so we can change the painful trajectory of history toward forgiveness, love, and the joyful celebration of women and their wonderful bodies.

On a soul level, when we choose to be female, (and I do believe we choose that) I profoundly believe it is because we are here to challenge the old paradigms. We cannot wait for the predominantly male powers that be to change: we must become the sources of our own liberation. It is my personal mission to help every woman accept this sacred truth. Burlesque can be alchemical in this sense. I have seen women walk into classes hiding their light and showing body language that does not affirm their greatness. By the end of class, those same women will have a spring in their step, a sway in their hips and an understanding that their body is worthy of celebration and that it can move in ways that can hypnotize and liberate in equal measure.

Ram Dass beautifully said that we are all walking each other home. Burlesque was my way home to me and my heart. It's not for everyone, and that's ok. Some folks simply aren't ready to be confronted with such honest and unapologetic beauty. Some aren't quite ready to recognize the sensual female form as something to celebrate, empower and support. We each have our own journey, and mine led me into far deeper truths and experiences than I ever could have anticipated.

I dedicate this opening chapter to three performers who I feel embody burlesque as a witness of the sacred feminine.

Julie Atlas Muz has inspired me from day one. A Whitney Biennial artist as well as an international touring performer, Julie's work blends the boundary between performance art and burlesque. Her style of dance is both intriguing and riveting. My personal favorites are her acts done to "You Put A Spell on Me", " You Don't Own Me", and "Breaking the Law" to name a few classics. Try to look away while Julie is performing, my bet is that you won't be able to, and wouldn't want to either.

Dirty Martini has consistently been voted the best burlesque performer in the world. Her jaw-droppingly gorgeous body and incredible technique are touchstones for me when I am working on an act or needing a spirited pick me up. Dirty is the first fan dancer in post-war Sarajevo, a pioneer of the neo-burlesque scene, a muse for the late Karl Lagerfeld, and a regular fixture on international stages. I bow to her and her boundless talent, charm, and beauty.

Ms. Tickle is originally from New Zealand and is an entrancing performer. She taps deeply into the energy of divine femininity in every one of her heart-stoppingly beautiful acts. She is the first performer to ever win three awards in the same year at the annual Burlesque Hall of Fame's Tournament of Tease (formerly Miss Exotic World). I am immensely grateful to her for bringing the sacred feminine front and center in all of her performances. We are all the richer for it.

TWO

The Myth of Separation: How Being "Not Enough" Led Me To Burlesque

*"Until you make the unconscious conscious,
it will direct your life and you will call it fate."*

—Carl Jung

G rowing up, my family attended church almost every Sunday. It was a sweet Episcopalian church called St. Mary's and I loved it very much. I remember the dark wood pews, the kind Father and his wife, the many sweet treats at coffee hour following the service. I can still see the hairstyle and bad suits of the Sunday school teacher who taught us every Sunday until I was old enough to rejoin my parents for services. The church was a place of comfort and community. As much as I hated waking up early on Sundays, I appreciated the rituals, singing and being able to look around and see the people I knew alongside each other.

When I was nine, something shifted inside me. I don't know what triggered it, but I came into a much deeper awareness of Jesus and what had happened to him. Seeing him on the cross was a regular sight, but I hadn't understood the violence, the depth and the sacrifice of that image and what it represented. A man gave up his life because of love and died in a cruel, unforgiving way. I took a small, private vow of silence for a day, overcome by a deeper sense of what had happened. It was the day before Easter, and I remember sitting at our dining room table - a heavy, old, carved wooden behemoth inherited from my grandmother. No one noticed my self-imposed vow, and I remember feeling very alone but also deeply committed to this new feeling inside of me.

The next morning we went to church for Easter service. I sat in those same dark wooden pews and opened the book of common prayer to join the congregation. In the aura of the deep feelings that had been swimming inside of me, the words I recited suddenly changed before my eyes. Instead of unity, I saw exclusion. This God was not a kind Father, at least not in the words I was reading. The prayers became judgment incarnate. They implied that some were more worthy than others of God's love and that not everyone was worthy of salvation. In that moment, I became hurt and deeply disillusioned. Why couldn't everyone be saved? Didn't God love us all equally? Why were some people "saved" and others weren't? It struck me as hypocritical. From that day forth, I said the prayers differently. Instead of the refrain, "Lord, hear our prayer," I started saying "Lord, hear their prayer." I loved the people around me but could not chant along with them. How could they so blindly follow these words, words that sowed difference and otherness in their fellow humans? Where on earth was Jesus' message of love? Had he died for nothing?

My life changed that day. No longer was church a place of love and safety. It became an ivory tower that excluded everyone who didn't fit into its strict parameters, and I wanted nothing to do with it. I developed a deep skepticism and resentment for the church, one that parlayed very neatly into my fury with male authority. Religion became associated with weakness, judgment, and separation for me, and I no longer wanted anything to do with it.

Many years later, I was able to revisit that moment with a deeper understanding. To be saved meant to accept the love of God/

Universe/Higher Power in your own heart regardless of religion, and accepting that Divine Love is a powerful embrace of true perception. We are all one, and nothing separates us from Jesus or Buddha or Allah or any other spiritual master except for our own resistance. I am grateful to have this awareness, and yet I can see how the word of God* has been twisted to suit both personal and nefarious ends with regards to those who hold power both in and outside of the church.

(* I use the word "God" here and moving forward because it is the easiest word to use when talking about the force that creates us all. I acknowledge the triggering use of the word for some and will go deeper into this in chapter five.)

To subscribe to "otherness" in any form is a gesture of belief in separation. To see anyone other than an equal is also an indication of a belief in separation. The exclusion that became so glaringly apparent troubled me because deep down, I knew that exclusion goes against the core message of love.

The belief in separation is a myth. The world around us, our society wants to show us constant examples of how separate we are. But if we just open our minds and hearts we will quickly see how false that is. We have never been separate from the other humans we meet, humans living a world away from us, or from all life on earth. The myth of separation has been told and reinforced since time immemorial, so it's understandable that we succumb to it. Overcoming the adherence to this myth is a journey attributed to heroes, saints, and Gods. The good news is, you don't have to be any of these things in order to embark upon this journey. You do have to be willing to dramatically alter your worldview (for the better) as a result.

When I was first confronted with this myth, I was equal parts fascinated and mystified. I could point to moments in my daily life where I witnessed the illusion of separation hard at work. Walking past a homeless person on the street, being single and looking for a mate, interactions with superiors at work: all of these observations and interactions were studded with a sense of inherent inequality. I was no more equal to my boss than I was to that homeless person. I was not worthy of the handsome men I so badly wanted to date, just as plenty of men weren't worthy of dating me. Everywhere I looked, I could see examples of how I was creating separation from everyone around me. I felt beholden to it and paralyzed by it. I subscribed to separation and made countless choices based on this foundation. I thought that paying into this system of hierarchy and otherness would somehow galvanize me, but it ultimately weakened me. Equality with others was not a consideration because it didn't fit into the conversation I was having with myself. When I finally accepted that my perceptions were deeply flawed, it was a huge reckoning.

How many times have you felt separate? While considering your place in the world, have you ever experienced feelings of separation or a feeling that you somehow don't fit in and are not worthy of inclusion or love? How many decisions have you made based on this idea? How did you feel after those decisions? Were they life-affirming or did they feel like you had to give something up (your values, an aspect of your identity, your sense of worth) to get there?

What if you could, from this point forward, believe that you are here for a reason and that reason is love? Would you be willing to accept that you deserve exactly what you want and that you are worthy of it without question?

This may seem like a quantum leap because for many of us it is.

For me, leaping into the belief that I was one with everything was initially as inaccessible as one of Jupiter's moons. My previous relationships and interactions had created a steadfast belief system that was anchored in separation. I was never good enough, never worthy enough and obviously unable to attain what I truly wanted in this life. When I finally confronted the possibility that my life could be based on inclusion/love/acceptance and not rejection, I felt as if a bomb had hit me. To boldly choose love wasn't an option

I felt I'd ever had. As exciting as it was, I confess, I was terrified to make this leap.

I still struggle at times with this truth, that I am equal to everyone around me and worthy of expressing myself as such. I'm human after all.

When I see how deeply attached people are to division and separation, I sometimes feel heartbroken or despondent. It can feel like an impossible mission to realign with that eternal sense of belonging and love. But it is a necessary mission. To counteract separation with the energy of love is daily work that keeps me honest. The programming of hierarchy and "otherness" runs deep through our individual lives and experiences. It is in our collective ancestral and emotional inheritances. It is up to us to challenge its prevalence by questioning why we continue to accept the myth of separation.

I want to offer you a new concept:

You have never been separate from who you truly are. You have and will always be surrounded by the force of love that permeates all life. Any belief that you are somehow separate and unlovable is a lie, pure and simple. The concept of separation is the greatest self-imposed con of the human experience.

Our shared perception of separation is a universal experience. We are told time and time again that we can't get what we want or need in the long run because life is hard, and it very much can be. I hear the stories of others and am humbled by what humans have done to each other out of fear, shame, judgment, and anger. Disconnection wreaks havoc. Most of us are not taught that our birthright is love and our sacred connection to one another. We are not shown that we are safe in the truth that we are loved no matter what. We are actively discouraged from knowing and trusting body wisdom.

Instead, we are taught to rely on logic and the power of the mind. We are taught that we have to strive in order to receive grace and love and that if we don't receive it that we are somehow unworthy or undeserving of it.

The ultimate goal of connection lies on the other end of a long journey back to ourselves. We don't have to wait our entire lives until we are on our deathbeds to get there. It is a truth we can tap into right here and right now.

When we experience connection with ourselves and our innate Divine spark, we experience fullness, intimacy, and a feeling of being seen and heard. Connection is the manna of human life. The most important relationship we will ever have is the relationship we have with ourselves. The wholeness we search for through the lens of other people cannot be found outside of ourselves. Only when we choose to connect to our own feelings and love can we begin to recognize and receive the reflection of the love in the mirror of others and our relationships with them.

The journey back to wholeness is the ultimate human quest. To move from a state of separation (head vs. heart, man vs. nature, internal vs. external) into one of unity and connection is the pinnacle of human experience. That sense of unity, be it sexual, spiritual or communal is what is at the heart of all human desire. It is what has always driven us and will continue to drive us forward into our many journeys and quests.

Human beings are relational beings. We need others in order to understand ourselves more fully. We see our reflection in the sacred mirrors of other people and through the relationships we have with them. The belief that we are somehow separate from everyone around us can provoke deep anxiety and feelings of uncertainty. A thought from the mind of separation may say, "if I have no one to reflect me back to me, do I even exist?" Our experience or perception of loss of connection creates isolation and loneliness in a vicious cycle that can continue endlessly unless we choose to stop it.

When we perceive a lack of connection, we create the thought that we are somehow not enough and unworthy of love. This is one of the most harmful inheritances of separation. We have been taught that we need others to love us in order to feel complete. We have been taught that our worth is dependent on the judgment of others. We attend religious services in sacred places and there we are taught that our human nature is impure, not to be trusted and that we are somehow all missing something at our core.

We are told to subscribe to a manufactured system of belief or in a higher power to expunge our record of errors and sins in order to be redeemed. These systems and religions rarely train us to feel worthy of our own trust and to know that we already have all the answers inside of us. Of course, there will always be questions to be asked, lessons to be learned and problems to be solved. But on this journey of realization and awakening, the most crucial learning device we have is our own connection to ourselves.

Why have we subscribed to a false version of reality for as long as we have? As horrific as the legacy of separation has been, I trust there is medicine in this question. My early experience of the human journey felt studded with signs that I was not enough, that I would always be separate from what I truly wanted because I hadn't done/been/accomplished enough. Separation sets us up for the bigger failure to recognize that we are born with exceptional, unique gifts and ways of interacting with the world. It refutes the fact that we are all actually here to support, love, and educate each other on levels way beyond our limited, loveable human form. The myth of separation attempts to doom us to an eternal cycle of disconnection. Therein lies a golden opportunity.

It's time to set this down and look at why we believe we are separate or unequal. There is a pervasive human thought that we are unloveable at our core. This is the ultimate human tragedy and yet, also one that offers a profound learning curve. The seeds of our collective redemption are in remembering that we hold a sacred union with all life.

"All learning has an emotional base."

—Plato

According to Jung's definition, "archetypes are ancient patterns of personality that are the shared heritage of the human race. Myths are populated by archetypes, and so it only made sense that I tapped into certain archetypes within the construction of my own personal myth. When I was confronted with the truth of oneness and unity, it forced me to look at the myths that I subscribed to in my own life.

My father represented the archetype of the absent male who had something I needed but could never possess: his presence, acceptance, love and nurturing. This played into my perception of all men; they all had something I needed in order to be complete, but they didn't stick around long enough for me to achieve that coveted feeling of wholeness. This thought made me both clingy and distant and perpetually unsatisfied, wondering why I couldn't find love.

My mother showed me the archetype of the devoted, all-sacrificing woman who had to do everything by herself with some help but little emotional support from those around her, from raising kids to running a household. This taught me that as a woman, I had to suck it up and settle for what life gave me. I grew up thinking there was some sort of martyred beauty in my elegant handling of my own disempowerment.

Within this formative archetypical pairing, I was steeped in a sense of deprivation. I did not receive the love of my father and therefore was wholly dependent on the love of my mother who was already stretched thin. I felt undeserving and unworthy of love. I felt that I would never be enough to win the charms or affections of a man or a loving community. I love my parents very much and am profoundly grateful to them for the life they provided for me. I am grateful too for their individual histories, including their traumas and their wounds. That wounding revealed a way home for me, a way back to my own heart as I negotiated and resolved my own wounds both experienced and inherited.

We are born independent thinkers, movers, and doers who are dependent on each other for survival. Human beings are highly relational creatures who need community, partnership, and networks in order to survive. We need to belong to groups without threatening the stability of them lest we ourselves become threatened with expulsion, abandonment, and rejection. These groups are our families, our friends, our religious, educational and shared-interest communities. No matter the group or how high its intention, herd mentality is real, and it is something we need to come into awareness of if we are to change and share more freely what lies deep within us.

Thanks to the myth of separation, we have allowed ourselves to become beholden to the thought that different is somehow bad, even punishable. The "other" is suspect because we don't know who they are. And for all we know, they could be here to hurt, kill or conquer us. This is a very old way of thinking that needs to be challenged more than ever. There is no "other." There never has been and there never will be unless aliens actually invade our planet and even then, it's arguable.

I remember going out to Coney Island, the legendary home of fun, fantasy, and freaks, for the first time. Coney Island warrants a pilgrimage. It is steeped in history and was home to America's first-ever amusement park. Given its location at the southwestern tip of Brooklyn, stories recount how immigrants headed to Ellis Island would first see the electric lights of Coney Island before laying eyes on Lady Liberty. What an introduction to their new life!

There is a famous sideshow and theater in Coney called Sideshows by the Seashore. This theater is home to the last fixed sideshow in the USA where you can find sword-swallowing, snake dancing, and human blockhead among others. Featured at the sideshow are the highly respected "natural borns" who are performers with physical anomalies often from birth. Here, difference is both celebrated and honored. It is a ripe ground for creative brilliance in an inclusive atmosphere that countless people adore (including me).

Difference does not constitute a threat. Other people, even if their entire body is just a torso, are just like us. They *are* us. They have the same needs and maybe even similar life experiences. If we have been trained to treat anyone appearing different from ourselves, separation is present and fear enters the picture. The word "freak" itself implies something strange or weird and can be used as an insult or tool of othering. We all have the same needs and desires and anyone who looks different from ourselves is just as worthy of love and inclusion as the rest of us. I love that these amazing freaks have the agency to earn an income, find a welcoming community and make a name for themselves with their wonderful, unique bodies.

Too often, however, different appearances can trigger fear which creates a cascade of problems.

When we buy into fear, we trigger survival thinking. This thinking comes from the limbic brain, whose sole existence is to preserve our life in the face of a threat. The tricky thing about our limbic system is that it takes everything personally, which is one of the reasons it has served us so well. If we perceive a tiger coming at us, the limbic brain makes us get out of the way as fast as we can and look for safety. If we perceive a threat to ourselves or those we love, we fight for their survival. This is an amazing gift and the prime reason why humans have made it through millennia up until this present moment. It can, however, complicate things when it comes to the ego, our false self, and its desire for survival.

The ego is our container, our individual personality that sets the boundaries of our personal expression. If you have spent any time with yoga or Eastern philosophy, you have likely heard about how we should work to renounce our egos. There is some truth to this, but I think the fundamental essence of why we need to eliminate our egos has been skewed.

If you view the ego as a "me me me" kind of thing, you are right. At its core, the ego is all about the individual personality and its expression. However, the ego is not necessarily a bad thing.

If the ego is a container, it begs the question: how much attention should we pay to the individual container and how much importance should we assign it versus the importance of the collective whole, which is made up of a chorus of personalities who have their own needs, all of which are equal to your own?

"We may ask how we could survive without our ego. Don't worry, it doesn't disappear. We can learn to venture beyond it, though. The ego is there, as our servant. Our room is there. We can always go in and use it like an office when we need to be efficient. But the door can be left open so that we can always walk out."

—Ram Dass

When people talk about how important it is to renounce the ego, to me it is an invitation to renounce the singularity of self. Each of us are unique and with gifts that are germane to ourselves, but there is no ranking system in the eyes of love. The ego loves to think it is the most important thing ever, but that thought alone is rooted in separation.

The message here is simple. None of us are more or less important than another. When we begin to break down the ivory towers that we have built around ourselves, we can experience real belonging and connection, the manna of human experience.

To believe that we are separate from all who surround us is the illusion of disconnection hard at work. Allow me to offer you a non-negotiable truth: you are never alone and you are never separate, period. You are eternally one with all you perceive, regardless of the egos and systems that try to tell you otherwise. The key to shifting your perception of this reality lies in your heart and in your willingness to try it out.

The heart is the seat of the soul, according to Traditional Chinese Medicine. TCM is the foundation of acupuncture, shiatsu, Tai Chi, and Wu Tao to name a few examples. There are other medicinal and spiritual traditions that also believe the centrality of the heart and how it connects us to ourselves. Home to our very essence, the heart has its own powerful consciousness and timeless wisdom that has very little to do with the mind. When we choose to sink our awareness down into our hearts, we find a deeper, more vast consciousness. The heart's capacity to love is limitless. When we consciously tap into this sacred muscle, this literal center of our being, we discover what our truth really is. The wisdom of the heart is ancient. When we act from our hearts, we animate that divine spark of our self into kinetic motion, giving form and expression to source energy, the very mystery that gives us all life.

When we accept the myth of separation, we create a rupture between our self and our source. It creates a sharp rift between the heart and the head. This illusion whispers to us that we are not equal, that we are not unified and that there is no way back to unity. Buying into this falsity, this break in connection-- that there is no redemption, no forgiveness and no possibility to ever return to happiness. creates discord in ourselves, our communities and our lives. Therein lies the rub. Separation is a lie. It's a myth. It is reinforced constantly, but is not what it seems.

Think, for a moment, about where separation exists in our lives and what systems it most profits. How many people use God as the grand divider? How many absolve themselves of any personal responsibility in their judgmental or unloving treatment of others? The canonization of guilt and shame has locked people into low systems of thinking that do not leave much room for love or a heart-based consciousness.

How can any of us be guilty or shameful if the love of God is our birthright? How can we remind ourselves that love, connection, and their inherent prosperity are in fact, our birthright?

We are living in a deep time of reckoning within the Church and its leadership. The revelations surfacing about the crimes and abuses at the hands of priests and the cover-ups perpetrated by the hierarchy of the Catholic Church shows us that the practice and enforcement of the myth of separation goes all the way to the top. At the same time, we see that humans are humans. We must practice love both within and without, knowing we too have our perfectly tailored lessons to learn, our own confrontations with accountability.

The trauma and pain of these times also provides us with a profound opportunity to step into a deeper reading of the essence of love. We can all be reunited with the truth of unity and oneness that has been ours from the beginning.

My own journey back to love has been a bumpy one. Ever since that transformative Easter day in church, I carried with me immense anger and a sense of injustice that felt far older and bigger than my young body. I felt emboldened by my rage and yet any time I began to share it, I felt horrible. I began to take out my unresolved feelings on those around me, on myself, and on my body. Despite my righteous-feeling anger, I wanted peace. I wanted to resolve these feelings that felt like fiery metal filings in my gut. The more I identified with what had happened to me, the thicker my walls around my heart grew.

When I was younger, I frequently slipped into despairing thoughts. If love was real, I certainly wasn't worth it, so what good was being alive at all?

Deep down I knew there was more to all of this. I just didn't know where to begin.

COMING HOME TO THE DIVINE

Soon after I started dancing full-time, I had to admit that I was struggling. For as much joy as my new path was affording me, I was aware that a deeper piece was missing.

Within two years of beginning my burlesque career, my life had shifted considerably. For as glamorous as I felt, and as excited as I was, I felt hopelessly stalled in old limitations as if I had hit a wall. How was I going to become a world-famous showgirl if I couldn't make a living? After a long, drawn-out sob session, a close friend introduced me to a healing modality called rebirthing breathwork.

This initiated a powerfully healing chain of experiences and events. I met the woman who is considered the mother of rebirthing breathwork. After an intensive weekend workshop, she and her fiancé invited me to India to visit their guru's ashram in the foothills of the Himalayas. It was part of a yearly pilgrimage during the Spring festival of the Divine Mother. For the first time in my life, I felt drawn to India.

I had a lot of preconceived notions about the country. I had always been equal parts fascinated and horrified by the subcontinent. My paternal grandmother had gone there on a Fulbright scholarship to study color therapy in her 50s. My father spent time there in his 20s buying and selling goods on the black market to support himself as he traveled across the world. It all sounded murky, strange and dangerous. I had no idea what was there and for most of my life, I didn't particularly want to go. My conception of it was that it was beautiful but poor with treacherous conditions, horrific overcrowding and filth like I had never known.

I was also very wary about the whole concept of the guru. It triggered all my old stuff about God. But despite the deep-seated discomfort I had with the concept of God, every cell of my body told me to take this trip. I experienced a massive financial miracle that allowed me to go, and off I went.

I made peace with God during my time there. I learned the power of surrender and forgiveness. I learned that being vulnerable was an amazing act of strength, not weakness. I saw so clearly how the universe is here to support me. I learned that the only thing holding me back from a sense of deep belonging to all of life was me. The experience was hard, uncomfortable and paved with lessons and experiences that held up a loving, unrelenting mirror that reflected the real me.

Yes, I am human. And yes, I have a perfectly imperfect journey with all of the relationships and lessons that came along with it. For the first time, I believed I was worthy of receiving and giving love. For the first time, I recognized that God was simply a grand YES answer to my thoughts and experiences. God became immense, eternal love. I bow my head in gratitude for the experience of falling apart and getting put back together again. I know that happened through the grace of God. I remain deeply grateful for the countless sacred reflections that revealed to me my true self throughout this journey back to wholeness.

While in India, I learned more about karma. I was very familiar with the refrain "karma is a bitch." I learned there that karma is only a bitch if you are. Karma simply means action. The concept of karma provides us with the human context for the law of physics that states every action has an opposite and equal reaction.

Another way to put this is, whatever you put out into the world will come back to you.

In the Vedic tradition, our actions in past lives play a role in our individual soul evolution. We are all born with karma, the reverberations of which echo down the halls of our lives and lineages. No two karmas are alike, and their threads tie us all together in infinite combinations and circumstances.

Given how my relationship with God and love evolved, I can only imagine my karmic history and present. I think about the way that the myth of separation has affected my life and the lives of my family and ancestors. I think about how my efforts around coming home to love and celebrating the gift of my body became my purpose. I surrender to the fact that I am still learning and will continue to do so until it's time for me to pass on.

DANCING FROM SEPARATION TO UNITY

Now, wherever I perceive the myth of separation, I see medicine for my heart. I do my best to walk with courage rooted in love to take the steps to mend the divide, sew the tear, and repair the belief that somehow we are not the same. When I catch myself buying into the thought that we are not one, that what is mine is mine and don't you dare touch it, I pause. Old habits and patterns take time to fully shift. I walk with forgiveness of myself. I forgive myself for ever having believed and taken action in the thought system of separation. I acknowledge the pain this belief has created in myself and in others. I can heal and soothe this pain of reckoning with my willingness to stand in the fire of truth. This is not an actual, physical fire, but the force of transformation that occurs when we continuously surrender our ego and false thoughts to the energies of resolution and unity.

In those moments, our ego is the only thing screaming out in pain. Our higher selves and our Divinity see the medicine in this fire and beautifully answer to the conditions we create so that we can grow, move and change.

The belief in otherness creates a deep-seated tension because deep down we know it to be untrue. When we see the eyes of another person, we are offered the privilege of seeing a reflection of our own Divinity. To attack another is to attack ourselves. Just as hate corrodes the container that holds it, our own feelings of disconnection from one another are the result of feeling that we are disconnected from ourselves and our highest good.

If we want to heal the divisions that separate us, we must look inward and find where we feel disconnected or divided within ourselves. We can only see in others what is already present within ourselves. We can only hate in others what we hate within ourselves. When we choose to love and bring that divine energy of union into our everyday lives, it has a powerful impact on our lives and the world.

This is what drew me to burlesque: it was a means of complete unification of mind, body, and spirit. My desire to move and express myself while adorned with fabulous makeup, hair, and costumes in front of a cheering audience was a windfall of joy for my soul.

Burlesque may be a unique way to connect to the Divine, but that journey home to one's self is not. There are as many other systems, tools, and stories as there are individuals. When present and willing, burlesque is a powerful tool to break down the beliefs of "not enough" and rebuild them into a more whole and sustainable sense of self.

The act of women coming home to their own innocence through the acceptance and love of their bodies is changing the world as we know it. Any form of art that harnesses the body, especially burlesque, is a profound and revolutionary demonstration of celebration and love.

Expressions of truth that challenge power structures are often seen and treated as deeply threatening. Those invested in that power have often sought to ruthlessly suppress it. This just reinforces how powerful art is. Art communicates with a part of us that does not need words. When performance art and burlesque enter the picture, an invitation to deeper intimacy and self-witnessing emerges.

We can only see what is already present within ourselves, and when we see a beautiful woman, man or genderfluid person claiming and expressing their joy, we are changed for the better. Watching someone expressing what is in their heart and their bones through physical movement is a viscerally powerful experience. It's especially powerful for someone who has never afforded themselves the opportunity to move, dance or create from this place of belonging to self. Witnessing these moments of expression can open new doors of perception. For some, their lives are never the same again.

If we can learn to approach life from this awareness of unity, oneness, and belonging, we can step into a deeper context of the structures and systems in our lives that have perpetuated inequality out of fear. Because our shared history in the myth of separation has resulted in deep intergenerational pain, it is increasingly important that we interrogate the flawed thinking that perpetuates this reflex to control and dominate, two pervasive tools of separation.

When we develop the willingness to go deeper into our own beliefs and experiences of separation, we can retrieve the truth and love that underlies our lives. We can begin to create healthy relationships to power that in turn create unlimited new possibilities for our lives. To paraphrase the theologian Richard Rohr, how can we release being fear-driven to becoming love-drawn? Spoiler alert: it all starts with your heart.

I dedicate this chapter to Jo Boobs, aka Jo Weldon, and Tigger!

Jo Boobs is the headmistress of the New York School of Bur-lesque and an unapologetic fox of a woman. Before coming into burlesque, Jo worked as a stripper and feature dancer in strip clubs for many years. She also is an advocate for sex worker rights and has worked tirelessly to elevate the visibility of sex workers and their deservedness of equal treatment. She has taught me to check what I am saying to make sure that it encompasses everyone, to leave out no one. She is the one who introduced me to thinking about the women on the margins, the whores, sex workers, and strippers, and how their journey and work matters.

Tigger! is the original king of boylesque (that's burlesque with a male tilt to it) whose colorful spirit and performances have entrenched him in the legacy and history of this art form. His generous, loving personality has very softly shown me to keep my shit in check. Many years ago, I lost a pair of shoes in a jumbled dressing room and I was convinced that someone had stolen them. Tigger very kindly told me that very likely I had misplaced them and to relax and look for them. I later found them at the bottom of my gig bag. I also honor his work in making gay male sexuality and sensuality a fabulous focal point from which we all benefit.

THREE

Hiding the Magic: Fear and Limitations of the Female Form & Feminine Energy

A ll of life is uncertain and humans have been fighting to survive for millennia. In many ways, it is a miracle we are here at all. Threats to human life from wild animals, disease, starvation, natural disasters, harsh elements, and other humans have been (and still are) frequent and unforgiving. In the face of the myriad of threats and uncertainties we have faced throughout time, humans have created systems to ensure safety and security in order to stave off the existential fear of death and destruction that paved so many of our ancestor's experiences.

Some of these systems are immensely helpful and help keep us safe and alive. For example, the stop sign. Its purpose is to prevent both accidents and death, and they just make sense. I am personally grateful for stop signs and obey them out of a desire to reach my destination safely. I appreciate it when others obey stop signs too. There is order in those signs that keep us safe and moving about our days.

Although laws like this and their enforcement have created frameworks for safety, order, and security, some systems of order have been designed to codify and enforce worth and are subsequently abused in order to sow the seeds of separation that enrich the few over the many. Modern-day systems of banking, government, infrastructure, and society were all built with elements of inequality. All of these systems function by separating humans into groups of haves and have-nots. It is these systems that we must pay close attention to because in their undoing we will establish and invest in the equal treatment and consideration that every person in our world deserves and so desperately needs.

Systems that thrive on inequality continue to have negative repercussions on marginalized groups. Judged by race, religion, creed, gender, sexual orientation, ability, income, and education (or all of the above), people are treated as though their worth and rights are dependent on what they look like, what they believe or who they love and surround themselves with. This farce of taxonomy is both outdated and harmful. It prevents us from connecting wholeheartedly with one another. It holds us back from a full understanding of our fundamental oneness, and it keeps us from seeing our fellow humans as equals who are worthy of the same considerations and treatments.

We can see the inheritance of these harmful legacies throughout our contemporary world. From racism to sexism all the way through to ableism and ageism (to name a few), too many times have the fundamentally incorrect and damaging perceptions of a few become gospel for many. I want to unpack this in a way to helps us re-assign responsibility to ourselves so that we can combat these destructive and oppressive reflexes that hide in the human psyche. Our goal is to retrieve wholeness.

We can look back in history books and read of African, American, Asian, European, First Nations and countless other continents and countries' histories of fighting each other and the invading, killing, raping and pillaging that comes along with it. This urge to dominate accompanied by cruelty has been with us since recorded time. It remains a brutal reality for millions of people.

Although history does not point to one sole culture uniquely responsible for the origin of cruel practices and conquests, the dominant, white, Eurocentric culture and global elite have profited handsomely in this long narrative of injustice. Western European colonialism, for us in the Americas, is the most recent iteration of this urge to conquer and exploit for profit, but examples of this are everywhere.

As a privileged, white woman living in the U.S.A., my experience of white, Eurocentric heritage is what I know best. I give deep thanks to my black, brown, queer, disabled, and freak friends who pried my eyes open to this uncomfortable and necessary truth. Like many people who look like me, I didn't know I needed to confront it, and now I can't look away.

Structural inequality inherently advances narratives of superiority to reinforce and justify oppressive practices that thrive on prejudice and power. When systems of rule and order have been designed with the thought that women, or people of color, or any other marginalized group are inherently unequal, the structure of that system will both bolster and warrant that the exclusions continue. How would that system be able to survive if its crucial tenets are shown to be built of smoke and mirrors? What happened for these systems to be in place? And why do we allow them to continue?

In two words, money and power.

The imposition of outside control upon land, resources, and people is an action that crushes freedom in favor of profit. It has been used since the dawn of time to force people to submit their bodies and sovereignty to an invading power.

By looking at ourselves and our own thoughts around separation, control, superiority, and power, we can develop a more trained eye and heart in order to cultivate a more mindful approach to the systems of power we subscribe to or buy into. In doing so, we can topple oppression from the inside out, dismantling their hold within us brick by brick. We can't change what's outside of us unless we change what's in us. That includes our inner adherence to these ancient and pervasive systems.

Let's look back 2,000 years when Rome and its army pioneered colonialism and the squashing and institutionalization of belief to benefit the state. It was the Romans who crucified Jesus and then later claimed Christianity as the official religion of the Roman Empire in a savvy move to tighten their grip on the populace they governed. Following several imperial edicts, ancient holy places were demolished and Christian churches built on their sites. This move not only destroyed the sacred sites of the ancient religions, but it also usurped the spiritual and symbolic power of these sites. In doing so, the Romans co-opted the power and significance of the older religions while simultaneously erasing the history that had cultivated and revered them. It was a brutal and effective move for them to create the consolidation of power they wanted. This is only one example of how the legacy of destructive decisions by those in power continue to impact our lives and consciousness to this day.

What have we inherited thanks to these dominating, militaristic cultures whose conquering impulses have flooded our lands and bloodlines? The legacy of these warlike cultures idolize the many legends and exaltations of the warrior and the belief that only the strong survive. Amid the pomp and circumstance is an inheritance that is neither glorified nor celebrated: the legacy of fear and trauma.

Trauma in one form or another has been part of the human experience since the dawn of time. So often we celebrate and deify the victor and relegate the victim or loser to the halls of shame and history. The controversial field of epigenetics studies the generational inheritance of trauma. It has provided fascinating examples of how children and grandchildren of trauma survivors experience the effects of events they never lived through. Although there is much debate about epigenetics, I feel it is a valuable lens through which we can view our inherited fear-based patterns. Whether the trauma is inherited or directly experienced, any resulting fear we hold in our bodies is holding us back from living our lives fully.

If we want to change the systems built on power and fear, we must understand how we have biologically adapted to respond and react to fear and why we allow it to call the shots. Whether we're running from a saber-toothed tiger or an invading army, or yanking someone we love out of harm's way, our fear and stress responses can mean the difference between life and death. However, when that reflex goes unchecked and we avoid higher thinking in favor of base, emotional reactions, we pay into a circular system of emotional reactivity that rarely brings closure or justice.

We can look to the great philosophers and peacemakers of history for different ways to approach sensitive situations where people on both sides of a conflict have unmet needs and are reacting in opposition to the other in order to meet those needs. We may have differences in life events or appearances, but we all have the same basic needs and the same biological and neurological wiring. As Maya Angelou said, 'We are more alike, my friends, than we are unalike.'

The fighting that we espouse and glorify is rooted in separation. If we are separate from each other and from God, how can we survive? Life becomes a constant struggle paved with threats and danger. But the truth is, we aren't alone. We have never been alone, and we have never been separate from everything that surrounds us.

LIMITING BELIEFS AND THE FEMALE BODY

Being born with a female body comes with a unique inheritance. For thousands of years, women have been told what they can and cannot do. Power structures have been and remain largely dominated by men and complicit women. Brave women throughout history have pushed back and rebelled against this limiting norm, and we are learning more about them every day as our collective consciousness seeks out their stories more widely. But the overall power and money-driven message has been for women to obey and be quiet. The limitations on women and their free self-expression were and are imposed by patriarchal cultures and rules. We must learn to peel off the layers of control and power heaped upon us, just as a burlesque performer peels off layers of costume to reveal their beautiful self.

My lived experience has been shaped by the fact that I have a female body. I was born female and identify as one. My body has been a source of celebration, income, and shame for me. It has been the canvas onto which I painted all of my internal strife. For the longest time, I felt that I was only my body. I was nothing apart from what I looked like. Sure, there was plenty more in there, but my looks were polarizing when it came to how I felt about my value and worth. My experiences taught me that beauty was celebrated, rewarded and monetizable but swiftly discarded when it faded. I bought into the idea that getting older meant a decrease in my value, and that was really scary.

I was born in the late 1970s in New York City and spent my early years in a very wealthy enclave just outside of the city. The dads of the families worked on Wall Street and almost all the moms stayed home. My elementary school was in a gorgeous, old mansion that had an extension built onto it to accommodate additional classrooms. Nearly everyone had a housekeeper and I thought it was perfectly normal to live in a house with six bedrooms and four bathrooms. Needless to say, my perception of what a "normal" life was like was quite skewed.

I remember lazy summer afternoons around the pool, surrounded by neighborhood friends and families: the laughs, the cocktails, the slicked-back hair of the dads, the hair, perfume and sparkly jewelry of the moms. I also remember when some of the dads suddenly had different women by their sides. What had happened to the beautiful moms? Where did they go? I learned early on about affairs, divorce and how some men would leave the mothers of their children for women who had younger, attractive bodies. I realize there was much more to what I was seeing, but that's what I took in. My memory holds that some women got fatter or older and that was somehow equivalent to them no longer being a welcome or valued member of the community. Beauty was a commodity, and everyone who had it was trading in it. To lose it meant rejection.

As I grew older and as my body matured, I attracted significantly more attention. This had a massive impact on me. The attention I craved when I was younger shifted from my ideas and spirit onto my body. I accepted that I had to rely on my appearance for a sense of worth and validation. I believed I was only as loveable as I looked. That was a lot of pressure to put on a young mind and body. Soon, I learned that I could get things I wanted because of what I looked like. My looks garnered attention, preferential treatment in stores, bars, restaurants and sometimes just walking down the street. I also looked great in clothes and was complimented frequently. I'm not going to lie, I really enjoyed it, but it came with a looming sense of inequality and that this was a temporary situation that would one day fade as my body got older. My relationship to my body and looks became one of "time is running out so I'd better use it while I have it."

It was utterly exhausting.

When I got into burlesque, I found myself surrounded by women of all shapes, ages, and sizes. It was mind-blowing to watch an older or heavier performer get on stage, strip naked and leave the audience howling and shrieking for more. I had never seen women value themselves the way many of my fellow performers did. I was used to allowing my thoughts of my own body to stop me dead in my tracks from getting what I wanted. If I didn't look a certain way, my self-talk and subsequent moods would take a dramatic downturn. Yet here beside me were women liberally applying glitter to their tummies and moisturizing their cellulite while chatting and laughing with fellow performers who were doing the exact same thing. The dressing room felt like a temple. All of a sudden I realized that what others thought of me, or the value they ascribed to me meant nothing. What mattered was how I felt and if I was happy with my performance. Nothing else ultimately mattered. That shift provided a profound and loving negation of a very limiting and obsessive pattern.

Apart from the regular, weekly shows that booked mostly everyone on the scene, I am certain that I was booked for higher-paid, glitzier corporate gigs because of how I looked. Yes, I used my slender, female, white body for my own advancement within the sparkling showgirl world. I booked modeling jobs, commercial gigs and even movies because of what my body looked like. I am grateful for all those experiences and the income they generated. But they also reflected back to me a chilling darkness. Were I to lose any of my beauty or slenderness, I would lose work and worse, I would lose any protections I had against deprivation, and that was terrifying. By the grace of love, I was able to ease these limitations out of my mind and heart and step firmly into the truth. The truth is that my body is enough as it is, as is everyone else's body that I come into contact with. Burlesque and all my sisters and siblings therein played a massive role in that. I learned there are no limitations upon our beings apart from what we place there ourselves and upon each other. And we can choose to be limitless.

What if these millennia of limitations originated simply so we can release them to the sands of time? No longer is the imbalanced male voice allowed to dictate our worth, our deservedness and our value. I think of the countless women all over the world, specifically in third world countries where they are still very much oppressed. From sweltering menstrual huts to female circumcision, there is a narrative of violence, suffering, and shame woven into being a woman, and it is rooted in disastrously limited thinking. It feels true to some because of the multitudes of complicit people who have enforced this untruth out of their own need to avoid fear and feel safe under the gaze of those in power.

It is time for each one of us to let these limitations pass away and for a higher truth to emerge. We are here to heal ourselves and each other. It's time to shed the weight of oppression by systematically challenging and pulling it out of ourselves.

We can only affect the whole if we begin with ourselves.

ROOTING OUT FEAR-BASED LIMITING BELIEFS

We are living in a powerful time of reclamation and uncovering of our deeper, core truths. From the rising voices of people who have not been afforded privilege or visibility, we are starting to demand more loudly and more immediately that everyone deserves equal treatment. We are starting to reckon with the fact that this has historically not been the case. There are many who do not want to afford gay, trans, indigenous, black, brown, disabled, female or "different" people equal rights or consideration.

The limited, fear-based nature of this position is one that is holding *all* of us back, not just the people targeted or suffering from lack of equal treatment. When we allow this conditional and limited thinking to dictate our decisions and treatment of others, we ally ourselves with a deep form of lack-based thinking which impacts every corner of our lives.

Here's how to put this in practice.

Ask yourself, "Do I hold fear-based beliefs in my life?"

Notice what comes up. Write it down if that helps.

Another way of asking this is, "Where have I let fear influence what I believe in?"

If this feels challenging, take a deep breath and remind yourself that you are on the ramp to a brand new highway of understanding. When we can begin to identify where we have allowed fear to create limitations in our lives, we can begin to undo them, one loving thought and stitch at a time.

If you are someone who acknowledges that "others" and their beliefs, appearances and life choices are weird or scary, I want you to play with and identify the root cause of this way of thinking.

Do you feel this way because someone taught you that different is bad?

Did someone tell you that whatever race/religion/identity you belong to is the best?

What else is there?

What did you receive or think up that has allowed this limitation to be there?

Please remember your connection to love as you navigate this terrain. Come back to the here and now and breathe into your heart if it feels like too much. The very personal work of rooting out deep beliefs is crucial so we can see our programming or beliefs for what they are, and shift them upwards into alignment with love.

We hold the keys to our own salvation, but if those keys are pink and covered in rhinestones and I'm strictly a black velvet gal, I have an opportunity to make a wildly limited decision that could significantly hinder the path of my life. You are a limitless being and we live in a limitless universe, so why bother limiting yourself? This life is yours to claim, celebrate and own outright. I am so excited for you to do so.

Stripping Off Limitations

Are you someone who is really hard on yourself because of your looks? Are you willing to consider that you can now choose differently? If in life you accepted the untruth that you are somehow unloveable, are you willing to unlearn it?

Have you ever called yourself or another ugly? Where was the ugly coming from? Was it material/physical ugliness or did it go deeper? Was it an emotional ugliness? Was it an ugliness that betrayed pain, or a feeling of worthlessness? Were you just viewing your own feelings of unattractiveness, of being unlovable, or self-disgust upon the canvas of someone with unconventional looks?

If so, some requests:

Please look beneath the pain, the fatigue, the traces of the well-worn path of time left upon the countenance of those you behold. Please look for the soul working its way through human life just like you, learning curves and all. Compassion is a beautiful thing and a necessary, nurturing need for us to navigate life trusting that we are loveable.

Working with affirmations can be a powerful way to counteract any negative thoughts or beliefs we hold about ourselves. Try saying the following out loud to yourself, and by all means please embellish, edit and rewrite them to suit your path!

I am unlimited potential.

I now release the limitations imposed upon me by others.

I now reclaim my worth and in doing so, I deepen the resonance of liberation on the planet for others to benefit from.

It is safe for me to be in my body.

I dedicate this chapter to the performers who embody the shedding of these beliefs: Perle Noire, Jezebel Express, and Darlinda Just Darlinda.

Perle Noire is the Black Pearl of Burlesque and an international star who has been captivating audiences since her debut. Perle speaks about how her very hard childhood showed her that there is no limit and that she can do anything she damn well pleases. Her fierce beauty and total control of the stage make her a powerful beacon of what is possible when we let go of limiting beliefs, pour our hearts into our work and allow ourselves to dance our truth. Her presence and work is a gift to behold.

Jezebel Express hails from Canada and I am so happy she landed stateside. Her work and advocacy for women doing their thing no matter what the patriarchy says, has been a touchstone for me when I come up against tough moments of self-criticism. Her brilliance both onstage and off is something I value very much along with her jaw-droppingly gorgeous body. She is one of the teachers at the New York School of Burlesque and I am so thrilled that she is one of the guiding lights for new performers.

Darlinda Just Darlinda is a powerful, potent lioness and excellent performer originally from California. Darlinda has been a beam of rainbow light for me. Her novel and amazing art projects (check out her Year in Rainbow) and her courage in putting together a one-woman show while performing full-time are so special to me. It takes serious balls to create work as nakedly (literally) as she does and I love that when I need a colorful pick me up full of love, there she is.

FOUR

Judgment: Releasing the Ties that Bind

*"We judge in areas where we are vulnerable
and the most susceptible to shame."*
—Brené Brown

Being human isn't easy. It's a hell of an assignment actually. We are born, expelled from the warm dark of the womb into a foreign, cold world. Our arrival often coincides with lots of noise and bright lights. As we develop and grow, our bodies become factories of hormones and chemicals that create emotional and physical landscapes. As we get older, we eventually hit adolescence and suddenly our bodies begin to change and develop in ways that we don't have any control over. Going through adolescence is a rite of passage that no one escapes if they're lucky enough to live through it. The sexual awakenings that happen during this time are natural and unavoidable, we are coming of age and preparing to be able to reproduce and further our species. This crucial stage of life is celebrated widely but is also policed by society at large. It's also a time of increased self-awareness, no matter how embarrassing it may be. The human growth process and awakening is a stunning journey but, boy, does it have its painful moments. Being human is messy and beautiful but it is easy to forget about the beauty when we are consumed by the viscerality and drama of our lived experience.

Part of being human is navigating emotional distress which is rooted in unmet needs. As we grow up, we have needs that demand to be met if we are to feel safe, connected and empowered. When those needs are not met, lower vibrations of fear, shame, and judgment enter the equation. When we believe we have a lack of safety, security, and nurturing affection, we develop fear. When we believe we are not worthy of acceptance, compassion, and validation, we develop shame. When we are deprived of support, guidance, and encouragement, judgment arises. We experience deep loss and hurt around our unmet needs. We are all negotiating various levels of these wounds. I choose to focus on judgment because it has been the most pernicious boulder in my grand hike through life. It has been the strongest force of resistance for me in my work to fully accept myself and others as they are.

A wise adage tells us "judge not lest we be judged." That's great advice not many people follow. I've met some people who do not allow their judgment to interfere with kind, equal treatment of one another. I've also met countless people who blindly cannonball through life, making decisions about how to treat others based on their judgments of everyone and everything in their lives.

Before I continue, I want to say that not all judgment is bad. It came in handy evolutionarily-speaking and in some ways, it serves us well.

Our ancestors used judgment to determine which wild foraged foods were safe to eat and which would kill them. They also needed to figure out who was a friend and who was a foe, sometimes in short order. This kind of necessary and helpful judgment is not what I speak of in this chapter.

I'm talking about the kind of judgment that brings heaviness in its wake, that weighs us down incrementally as we desperately try to pawn off the unbearable weight onto someone else. Our ancestors passed these reflexes along to us. As life has become safer, we have to balance the vestiges of evolutionary judgment. We have to be careful about how we use this skill of survival when we judge and assign value to people and things and treat those judgments as real facts that carry weight.

What I speak of in this chapter is the kind of judgment that has no bearing on reality.

What I'm suggesting we dismantle has everything to do with self-aggrandized opinions and little to do with life or death reality.

Judgment has landed us squarely in the majority of the social issues we face today. The belief that any person, group, idea, belief or system is better than another, or that one group has more rights than others is a lie put in place. Someone or some group benefits from this lie. Those external, imposed value systems are based on strictly limited perceptions that do not attempt to encompass the enormity of love and possibility that lies outside limited thinking.

This is a corner of our collective psyche that desperately needs healing. The archetypes, the stigma, the history, it all needs to be pulled apart and re-examined through empowered, loving eyes. We cannot solve the problems we are facing without deprogramming ourselves of judgment so that we level the playing field and create new possibilities for ourselves and our world.

Despite my best efforts, hours of therapy and lots of applied work, I still find myself judging others. Re-educating this deep, learned behavior has been one of the steepest learning curves in my healing journey. Some of my most painful learning experiences happened when I believed in my own judgment about a situation only to discover the truth. The two things, shockingly, did not match. The humbling reality of shallow thinking and arbitrary assignment of value is a bitter pill to swallow. This kind of medicine doesn't always feel or taste good, but it is necessary to take if we wish to improve our mental and emotional health while creating new possibilities that lie outside of our known comfort zones.

I was trained from an early age in the fine art of judging others. I learned through example and by overhearing people talk that we all exist in an invisible hierarchy. Watching the conduct of others,

I saw that other people were either more or less than me. I learned I had to protect myself from judgment lest I be dragged into the morass of that horrific, inescapable vortex. The thoughts that either created or resulted in judgment seemed to have serious weight to them. Why otherwise would people pass judgment all the time and make decisions based on those thoughts? There are a select few people whom I have met that have seemed either impervious to judgment-based criticism or have risen above it, but they were few and far between. I admire those people endlessly.

I attended an all-girls school for eight years during which time I went through adolescence. I loved my single-sex education but it also meant being thrown into a tornado of inevitable comparisons and projections as we all matured and developed at different rates. It was a brutal time, and although I was fortunate to have wonderful friends, I was also introduced to the cruel beast of judgment at a much steeper pitch. Entire friendships could catastrophically end because of it, and given the whirling hormones and the newness of certain relationships, judgment was both a weapon and armor to be used as needed. Drastic new behaviors or opinions could be justified by it. Something arbitrary could be transformed into something essential only to be switched back again. No one seemed to know their true north. Some girls were certainly better at speaking truth to nonsense but I was not one of them. For as boy-crazy and curious as I was, my whole experience was tinged with shame. I feebly attempted dominance in the face of others' judgment and inevitably failed, piling more shame onto myself. I felt doomed to the eternal cycle of being a nobody, thrown into a hot topic of gossip and back again. It was a horrible, hopeless feeling that I tried to squeeze out of by using bizarre and problematic logic to feel better about myself.

Having grown up in affluent corners of New York, I was accustomed to the unspoken guidelines and qualifications necessary to be deemed acceptable and worthy of polite society. To invoke jealousy was an odd kind of jackpot because it meant I possessed an item or attribute of value according to someone else. My experiences at that point did not teach me that I was enough as I was. The thoughts, feelings, and opinions of others had an impact on my sense of worth and identity. I partook in the reckless and arbitrary convictions of others with little regard to the effect these thoughts would have on the people they were aimed at. When the tables were turned, I was devastated. How could people think such horrible or untrue things about me? Worse, they knew and believed the lies I believed about myself; that I was ugly, unworthy, and/or a horrible person. It hurt but didn't stop my reflex to indulge in the judgment of myself and others.

When I lived in England during graduate school, I noticed an innate reflex of the English to classify people in order to assess their value or standing. When I realized this default taxonomy of value and identity, it made me approach conversations differently so I could more swiftly be accepted into polite society and not be ostracized or confined to the edges of social acceptance while others talked about me. I had never seen classification and social sorting laid so bare before. Everybody practiced this categorization with immense gravitas. I was acutely aware of wanting to land on the "right" side of judgment. I had experienced that "othering" in elementary, middle and high school, and it had been immensely painful. I wanted to avoid being negatively judged and yet still I participated in that vicious system so that I could feel better/prettier/more valuable than someone else.

I think that is why the words of the third judge in my amateur burlesque debut stung so hard. I stepped out with my heart on my sleeve only to be told that I wasn't very good. Ouch. I'm grateful I can now let that go and know that I was doing what I could with what I had on little notice. Not only was I enough within that moment, but I was also completely lovable, screw-ups and all.

Here's the simple truth as I have come to understand it. People can only see in others what is already present within themselves.

Looking back, I now see how the girls in school who judged me were simply showing me their own beliefs about themselves.

Nothing I ever did had anything to do with who they were as people and vice versa. I shudder when I think back to some of the nasty things I said about others and that others said about me. It was like we were throwing poop at each other. All we did was get ourselves dirtier and smellier and become more desperate to take a long, hot shower to wash it all away.

You see, judgment is rooted in separation. It assigns value and meaning to people, things and events that are arbitrary and conditional. One exception is the court of law, but that is an arena where the importance of a balanced and fair judge is brought into stark contrast against the backdrop of life-and-death decisions that are taken there.

This is not a chapter about law and courts, but I will say this: the criminal justice system is in desperate need of reform because of the judgments of people who created and perpetuate the system as it is. Because of petty human judgment, laws exist that discriminate and/or hobble minorities, poor people and anyone else deemed "other" and thus unworthy of human rights and protection by the ruling powers. This also includes women making decisions about their own bodies and using their bodies however they wish. We have the triad of fear, shame, and judgment to thank for racism, sexism, homophobia, ageism, ableism, and every other limited thought that we hold to be true. This impulse to categorize and arbitrarily assign value is one we must vigorously question and challenge if we are to progress as a people and species.

Why do we judge? What purpose does it serve? When we begin to cultivate vigilance, we begin to see where the roots of judgment lie. When we get down into it and see the inherent falsehoods those judgments are based on, we can release ourselves from the bondage of them. We can develop healthy relationships with our own sense of power and duty. When we let go of judgment about ourselves, we can get out of our own way to accomplish the work that is ours to offer in this life.

As souls in human form, we are acutely aware of limitations. We can only perceive what is available to us through our six senses and this time-bound, finite form (a.k.a. the body). We have no reference point outside of our own lived experience. As a result of this limited perspective, we can only see in others what is already present within ourselves. It is hard to recognize and embody love or kindness for someone who has never known such things. I have found that judgment tends to point to inner pain and strife.

We are each deeply worthy of love simply because we are here! If we could all innately remember that holy truth, our world would change overnight. Instead of looking at each other and seeing what we can't stand about ourselves, we would be able to see each others' right to be as we each are, learning curves and all.

Anyone who viciously attacks, judges, or legislates against a specific group of people based on where they're from, what they look like or who they love is projecting their own shame onto those groups and do so with vituperation. The thought that *I must somehow punish others so that I no longer have to see my own reflection that I despise* is a chronic illness that flares up in humanity time and time again, whether individuals are conscious of it or not.

I think about all of the conservative religious leaders, congress, people, and heads of institutions who condemn certain behaviors only to be discovered perpetuating the same acts behind closed doors themselves. How much of what a person says is a reflection of the person saying it? Look at the closeted gay politicians who rail against homosexuality and then are caught with a same-sex lover or prostitute. Or look at religious figures whose abusive behaviors violated members of their congregation. If they are caught with their pants down, it all-too-often gets swept under the rug. Or they are publicly shamed and it's game over for them and onto the "pleading for mercy" phase if they want to recover any sense prestige given to them by the group they belong to. How totally exhausting and unnecessary.

This rigid system of morality is both suffocating and outdated and it is consistently contradicted. Why do we retain these ancient systems of judgment, polarization, and prejudice when they clearly no longer serve us?

We hold onto them because the people who have historically been in power need us to do so. Their power and control over people rest on our own persistent judgment that reinforces our own illusions of inferiority and superiority and keeps us boxed and locked into our own limiting beliefs.

Undressing Judgment—An Exercise

Imagine you are confronted with someone who sends your judgment into overdrive. Perhaps you are triggered by their looks, their body shape, their skin color, the way they speak or any mannerisms they may have.

Bring that person to mind and notice all of the thoughts you have about this person both positive and negative.

Once you have that list complete, scan it and honestly notice what that person is reflecting back to you that you cannot stand about yourself.

If you're judging their body, how do you feel about your body? If you're judging their spending, how's yours? If you are noticing a mannerism or habit that drives you up the wall, what is driving that strong dislike within you? Is there anything in your life that you are not taking responsibility for and instead projecting onto another person?

Are you willing to close that destructive loop and plant yourself firmly and lovingly in front of the mirror so you can see what really drives this impulse to judge another? In the rocky terrain of judgment, all roads lead back to our own relationship to ourselves.

The toughest inheritance of judgment is that it limits our own appreciation of ourselves. It creates barriers to the healthy flow of energy throughout our lives. To judge is to hold an energetic grudge. If the person we are judging has harmed us in one way or another, the grudge may run very deep and the attachment to it may feel like a righteous and stable foundation. In truth, it is more like a cement casing that keeps us locked in place, unable to move or progress.

So how do we minimize the presence of judgment in our lives? One quick way is to step into discernment, which can be defined as the practice or action of figuring out what stays and what goes without polarizing judgment. Discernment can be practiced both logically and intuitively. The practice of discernment makes space for neutrality, which allows us to figure out what is in our best interest to retain or release from our lives.

When I began dancing regularly, I was assailed with my own judgments of others. I wanted to be friends with everyone because I had found such belonging, but when someone didn't return my affections, I would shut down and dive into judgment as a way of making myself feel better. Backstage, if anyone shared anything that I found problematic, I would slide deeper into judgment and resentment instead of challenging them in a loving way. Sometimes other people wouldn't have to say a word. All they would do is walk into the dressing room and my hackles would go up, along with emotional walls that prevented authentic connection. No matter how righteous these judgments would make me feel, if I ever shared them with anyone else and was challenged, part of me would collapse when I saw how harsh and unnecessary these thoughts were. Instead of taking full responsibility for whatever the other people were reflecting back to me, I mired myself in a smelly swamp that stained and soiled my emotional energy. I froze myself from progressing or having difficult conversations because deep down, I was terrified that my own horrible stuff would come out and I would be rejected. It was much easier to stay removed in my own ivory tower of judgment that kept me separate and shut down.

The hardest target of my judgment was my own body. This got thrown in my face hard when I would see heavier, or older performers get up on stage. I would try to love what I saw, but my own self-hate kept me trapped in judgment. It wasn't until I saw a larger performer get up and knock the socks off of everyone in the room while championing and celebrating their own body that I had a massive revelation. Every body matters on that stage because they each house an utterly one-of-a-kind spirit. Each and every body I saw became a messenger for me to love myself more completely. As I admitted my faults and limitations, I experienced immense love that permanently altered my vision. I am so wildly grateful to my sisters, brothers, and siblings of fluid gender and their unique, amazing bodies for showing me who I am: someone worthy of love and someone very much worth celebrating.

It makes it easier to write people off, belittle or reject them when we feel that they are somehow not worthy of our admiration, acceptance, and affection. It helps us avoid our own feelings in these moments. We don't have to look at our own pain or spend any time with our own feelings if we are busy staring out the window and judging everyone and everything left, right and center. To dig our heels in and cling to our judgments is a grave disservice to our fellow humans. Instead, we can begin to see their humanity and foster compassion for their choices in life. Everyone is loveable and the more we look into our own issues with love, we can begin to perceive that we are all on a large learning curve called life, doing what we can with what we have. There is always room to grow. When we give ourselves permission to have a fully human experience and love each of our mistakes and errors, we create fertile ground to grow taller than we ever dreamed and offer the same support for each other.

Undressing Judgment Questions

If you have a judgment about the human body and it's worth and expression, are you willing to set it aside while you read these pages? It's not required, and if you cannot, that's okay. Please know that whatever comes up for you is worth paying attention to. Are you willing to allow some love in as you feel your way through it?

There is room for everybody in this messy and crucial negotiation, you and your thoughts included. You have permission to go there and be freed.

How often do you judge others?

How much energy have you expended on judging another person, situation, relationship? Are you aware of how much energy, effort, and oxygen you spend judging others?

What is judgment holding you back from?

If you were to suspend judgment, what would become possible?

Are you willing to see the beauty in whomever you are perceiving? Can you see how it is easier to create more allowance and acceptance of your own humanity by suspending judgment?

What are your most deeply held dreams and beliefs?

Notice the first thing that comes up.

Now notice what stands in between you and it.

What will it take to get you out of your own way? (I'm writing this for myself as much as I am for you, dear reader!)

Bring a successful person to mind—a person you can't stand.

What is it about them that you do not like?

What are they reflecting back to you about yourself?

Are you willing to shift that perception and allow in the love and growth that your judgment is blocking?

JUDGMENT CAUSED BY THE MYTH OF PERFECTION

Perfection is a beautiful thing to behold. A freshly bloomed flower. Light refracting through a crystal. The love in our hearts and on our planet. Do you know what isn't perfect? Humans. We may have perfect hairdos or perfect records of conduct, but we are so profoundly imperfect that to strive for it is a fool's errand. Of course, working to be as well presented as possible has its benefits, but the judgment underlying it that suggests "only perfection is acceptable" is the problem.

This pervasive myth of perfection has plagued humankind for far too long. It certainly plagued me for decades. How many times did I stop myself dead in my own tracks because what I was doing or being was not enough and thus not perfect? What an impossible standard! The need to be perfect, to have all the answers, to be in control no matter what, may seem like a foil for acceptance but is a need to be separate. It says, *I cannot be seen as an imperfect human because that is not acceptable and thus not lovable. My learning curves and negotiations are not acceptable because they are a sign of weakness. I have to cover this up at all costs and use judgment as a shield to defend and protect myself.*

Whoah! Harsh, right?

Our flaws may be uncomfortable to perceive but they also are an invaluable learning tool. They shape the lens through which we behold our perception of life. For me, the centrality of my own relationship with my body has carved out steep learning experiences for me, ones that guided me back home to love of myself and of my process. Everyone is going to have their own unique lens and process, but we are conjoined in this process of unlearning by the presence of love that drives it all. This is why it's so important to show up for each other. When we are offered a loving reflection of ourselves in the mirror of our friends, family, and coworkers, we can unlearn and let go a few more of the untruths we hold to be self-evident.

Flawless is neither human nor possible unless you are a gem or geometry. By accepting that you are a flawed person who is bound to make mistakes, you can free up an enormous amount of energy that was dedicated to policing and investing in your own myth of perfection.

You have never been perfect and you never will be.

Perfection belongs to the realm of Divine Intelligence and the Universe. It is not something humans can be, strictly speaking. It is not our job to be perfect. That's up to God and no one else.

What sweet relief to let it go and just be.

Undressing Judgment Question

How many times has criticism of yourself slowed you down, or even stopped you dead in your tracks?

What if you instead asked yourself:

"Am I willing to love myself with all my faults and failings?"

Notice how that feels. Offer yourself the awareness that people can only see in you what is present within themselves and begin to pick yourself back up with this awareness. Walk with this, and repeat as needed.

JUDGMENT CAUSED BY THE MYTH OF MASCULINE VS FEMININE

Gender is a pervasive tool of separation. It is time we paid closer attention to why we attribute value and meaning according to biological or chosen genders.

If we are to proceed with the intention of unity and love, we must begin to accept that gender is a social construct, just like race. Yes, there are plenty of female-identifying women and male-identifying men, but what about effeminate men? What about masculine women? What about the people who don't conform to binary gender norms and who play with their self-expression through the spectrum of gender? Are they no less worthy of love and acceptance than you are?

Whether we are born male or female, those words mean nothing more than what we ascribe to it. Historically, men have wielded more power than women. They have been the lawmakers, the landholders, and the leaders. Their voices, stories and accomplishments dominate our history books. There are plenty of women who broke the molds that society tried to squeeze them into, but their stories are unfortunately few and far between.

The age-old, worn-out stereotypes, would have us believe that men are the providers and women are the sustainers. Whereas women are the glue that holds families and societies together, they have been told and taught to serve, rather than lead. Outside of a relationship to a man, women have been (and still are) treated as if their voices and presence do not matter. I shudder at the limitation of this view.

I'll use the example of fairy tales. These stories are told and retold and embedded in young psyches regardless of gender roles and expectations therein. So many of our well-worn stories center around the princess's sole quest to find her one and only prince. The princess isn't shown as someone with autonomy and power, but instead as a pawn in greater systems of power whose worth is determined by the holdings of her father. She is not a wild woman beholden to only her own heart, she is property and a prize. I find this archetype completely depressing and highly limiting. How many little girls have been taught this archetype as something to emulate? How about the little boys who began to believe that it was their job to save others because they were too weak to stand on their own? How many little boys read the example of the prince only to compare their own life experiences back to this archetype and realize that they had somehow failed?

Now apply everything I said about gender above to the narrow definitions of worth that have resulted in ableism, ageism, racism, classism, homophobia, religious prejudice, and sizeism. I am sure there are more ways that people have been prejudiced against, but this is a good place to start.

If you choose to work through your own beliefs about anyone who lives at the intersection of one more of these "isms" as somehow limited, please remember to walk with love. It may not be easy or comfortable, and that is okay. Love surrounds you as you learn and grow. When we can more easily recognize and see equality in each other, the kinder we can be to ourselves as we navigate our relationship to others and otherness.

Think of all the people you've known in your life thus far. Have you met feminine and masculine women, or any feminine or masculine men, or any trans people? Perhaps you have witnessed humans who possess a fluidity of expression of their unique, innate energies in their sovereign, human body. Of course, it may seem natural and pre-determined that men are masculine and women feminine, but I believe this to be a grave error in perception. It doesn't mean that women aren't feminine and men masculine, far from it. If anything, each energy has its own subtle expressions wherein the energies of giving and receiving, night and day, dynamic and submissive play out in infinite ways in our lives. There are times and situations where I feel both my masculine and feminine energies playing out in their own times and ways. I am grateful to let them flow without thinking twice about them. I realize my immense privilege in this and I hold space for all to be able to express and play with their self-expression safely and freely.

My burlesque community introduced me to the conversation around gender that we are now increasingly having on a national and international scale. I consider it a great privilege to witness the beautiful, crucial and huge exploration of gender identity of many of my fellow performers. Biology is one thing and gender identification is another. I am in awe of anyone who ignores what society or scripture has to say about who they are and how they should be or dress. It doesn't matter if they're a man or a woman or something else entirely. What matters is that they are living their lives according to what brings them joy and harming no one in the process. If only we were all so brave.

GOSSIP: A HARMFUL PERPETUATION OF JUDGMENT

We've discussed strategies to dispel judgment, but there is one way we can drastically cut down on our engagement with this heavy energy. It is rooted in how we treat each other and more specifically, how we talk to, and about, each other.

There are certain needs and behaviors of humans that are shared universally, and one of those is the need to know. The byproduct of this need is gossip. Idle chit chat, speculative stories both alleged and true, gossip is the fastest way to promote and reinforce judgments. When we curtail our urge to gossip, we can create meaningful change in our lives and in our emotional well being.

A favorite pastime of most human beings, gossip is the currency of social leverage. It is what we see plastered all over magazine covers at the supermarket. It drives reality television. It thrives on social media. It is a weapon used to invoke fear, shame, and judgment and imbue its spreaders with a kind of power or know-it-all-ness. Gossip can take on its own exponential dynamic while each person who spreads it gets tainted by its corrosive energy.

I personally used to love gossip. It felt great. I loved finding out a juicy morsel of news and spreading it widely and wildly. Gossiping about people made me feel like I had some sort of power, authority, or importance, which I did have but not from sticking my nose and opinions into the lives of others.

The sour fruits of my gossiping came back at me with some very uncomfortable, dare I say painful, consequences. On several occasions, I had to face the impact of my gossiping as I was told in no uncertain terms exactly what the people I had been gossiping about thought of me. My ego was repeatedly crushed when that happened, and rightfully so. After all, the ego's job is to separate us from all that surrounds us, including our friends and neighbors.

The ego and its justification that says I am more important than anyone else gives us a great incentive to divide and create expansive rifts between each other while we focus on how different, shameful or (fill in the blank) another person is. Again, that separation is an illusion. We do unto others what we do unto ourselves. You are ultimately the person you are gossiping about. When we gossip, we drink the poison of self-contempt. By partaking in it, we deny ourselves the consciousness and experience of unity that is always present.

Another product of gossip is the erosion of trust. I know lots of people who gleefully gossip and it keeps me from sharing my most intimate and personal things with them. Why would I share what is confidential with someone who is going to proverbially plaster it all over Times Square? No thanks.

Gossip represents a lack of integrity. It is one big energy leak. When we engage in gossip, we contribute ruinously to our own wellbeing. Culturally, when we spill the tea, we would do well to clean it up quickly and come back to ourselves and take care of what's up for each one of us instead of continuously scalding each other with words.

Stripping Down Gossip Questions

Think about someone you know who gossips a lot.

Is this person happy or satisfied with their life?

Do the energies of deep contentment resonate in their being? Would you feel comfortable sharing your truth with them knowing that it would not be kept safe?

When you gossip, how does it feel in your body? Do you notice an effect on your heart or nerves? How about when you hear gossip? Is there anything substantial to gain or earn through spreading it?

Are you willing to abstain from gossip? How about for three days? Or a week? Longer?

Dressing Up Discernment

Does what I want to share help the person I want to dish on?
Will it have a positive impact on their lives and on the lives of whom I am sharing this with?

How does the spreading of this make me look? (it can be useful to cue vanity in these moments to stop malice in its tracks.)

It is immensely important to be vigilant in our conduct if we want to create meaningful change in our communication and our lives. Just as a pebble dropped in a pond creates a replicating array of ripples, your words create reverberations far beyond yourself. All thought is creative, so which words do you choose to speak into reality?

A great antidote for judgment is to begin each judgmental statement with "I feel," such as, "I feel that Person X is putting themselves in danger by associating with Person Y." By doing so, you take control of your own feelings about what's going on and afford your subject autonomy from your opinions.

Another great way to practice kind communication is to listen. There is a practice called compassionate listening, wherein a person shares whatever is going on. For a set period of time, the listener does not speak. This powerful exercise allows people to be heard and seen while working through situations that they need an ear to help process. I also recommend reading about non-violent communication, a powerful way to connect and communicate with others. Marshall Rosenberg created this work and it has greatly influenced how I engage with others during difficult conversations.

Another way to bring more integrity into your communication and halt the harmful spread of gossip is to keep private any news that is shared with you. When we practice that integrity, it fortifies our energy and authenticity. We can also set ourselves up well when sharing sensitive or private information by saying "This stays between you and me. Please don't share this with anyone." This is a great way to create safety with clear boundaries in place.

Although we can't stop the human urge to judge, we can monitor our own engagement with it. The more vigilant and committed we are to our own integrity, the more we can loosen our need to judge and allow more room for love.

FORGIVENESS

Oh, forgiveness. It is the highest and hardest thing any human being can do. When I first started learning about forgiveness, I was told that it is the "master erase." When we forgive, we release our attachment to a person, event or moment that we feel has harmed us. Have you heard that wonderful saying, "let go or be dragged?" To forgive does not mean to forget. Forgiveness releases us from the burden of resentment and unresolved emotion so that we can be free. We may remember the relationship or event well into old age, but we are no longer beholden to the emotional baggage of it. It becomes a dot on the map of our soul journey with no residue left behind.

Forgiveness is brought about by our ability to call in the presence of love so that we can release ourselves from any emotional ties that bind us to our past. It is a powerful antidote for anger, rage, and resentment. I firmly believe this is one of the reasons Jesus made such an impact over his short life. He preached forgiveness and love, two of the hardest things we can undertake in the face of pain, anger, and grief. It is one of the most difficult things any of us can undertake in a lifetime. Despite the terrain and time required to fully forgive, the reward is reaped in increased lightness, feelings of freedom and a clean slate for us to begin anew and make new choices anchored in love and integrity.

Shimmying Into Forgiveness

How do you feel about forgiveness? Do you think or feel that it is possible?

If you were to completely forgive someone, what would your life look like?

If a person, relationship or situation comes to mind, here is a powerful exercise I learned from my teacher Sondra Ray and her amazing book *The Only Diet There Is*:

I, _____, completely forgive (person/situation/event).

Write or repeat aloud 70 times per day for seven days. Brownie points for practicing this for 28 days.

This crazy thing called life isn't easy. When we can pull back our harmful reflexes to judge and stop spreading damaging energy that is out of sync with integrity, we can begin to see a freer, easier path appear before us. We are each other's mirror. Are you willing to allow all roads to lead back to the love that you want to cultivate for yourself? When we bless our mirrors with compassion and deeper levels of understanding of the human journey, we free ourselves from the prisons of lower thought and begin to pave our way into incredible new possibilities.

I dedicate this chapter to the burlesque performers who are doing the hard work of leveling up. The burlesque community, like many other current artistic groups and communities, wrestles with issues of identity, privilege, ownership, and being respectful of one another's bodies, ideas, heritages, and cultures. I deeply appreciate the courage and integrity of the performers who are speaking up with truths for us all to face. I salute and acknowledge the many performers who are admitting they have work to do and begin to do it. To those who are actively engaging in the work of looking inside and changing thoughts and actions to more love, compassion, and kindness, this is for you. Burlesque will become more beautiful the more we show up and do the hard work.

FIVE

Burlesque as Medicine:
The Revolution Starts Within

We as humans on planet Earth are working through a new evolution of our hearts and minds right now. As the social systems we have known and used for years begin to show their outdated and limited nature, we have a powerful opportunity to create a new movement borne out of love and each one of us, one at a time.

Burlesque is a revolutionary art form. No other avenue of artistic expression relies so completely on the empowered, unclothed female form where the women themselves call the shots. We see throughout popular culture the power of female beauty and sexuality. Typically it is held up as an impossible ideal to chase or a commodity that can be bought or sold. I am grateful that we live in a time where this is changing, but there is still work to be done and progress to be made. When a woman feels full and complete in her being and authority, she doesn't need to excessively buy anything. Think about how many companies prey on her feelings of lack that drive her desire to acquire beautiful things that clog her home and her life. Her personal and professional relationships change as she steps onto equal ground with everyone she meets. She no longer pays into a system that relies on her subservience or indebtedness and instead allows her choices to be enriching personally, no matter how challenging or difficult they may be. When a woman stands fully in her power and decides to say "enough," the battles and fights we face will drastically reduce.

This level of self-assurance and clarity of vision is what the crones and hags of yesterday and today know so well. These older women and their wisdom have been systematically downgraded, insulted and stripped of meaning and value throughout the ages. Their wisdom and experience found threatening to fear-based male power. It is time for us to reclaim them and their powerful gifts as we resurrect their worth and value. When we allow the wisdom of older women who have lived and loved for many years into the lives, minds, and bodies of younger women, we will fundamentally change the world.

When the women who have been told that they are not enough come to realize that they have been lied to and that they are in fact more than enough, those false beliefs will give way to awareness and change. In order to retrieve our fundamental truths, ones that have been obscured and oppressed, we must choose to embrace ourselves with unconditional love. We trust the truth of our inherent "enoughness".

There is truth in the words of Gil Scott-Heron when he proclaimed: "the revolution will not be televised." This is a revolution that begins quietly, in our homes, in our hearts, in our daily interactions. It is revolutionary to simply decide to love and celebrate ourselves as we are. When we stop paying attention to external valuations of who we are based on what we look like or what we do, we get to create a new code for ourselves, one that is deeply rooted in love. This is a wildly infectious process because how we treat ourselves easily becomes how we treat one another. This is how the revolution begins.

If we look at the inheritance of patriarchal systems of thought and value, we can clearly see what (and who) has been deemed valuable and useful and what hasn't. The female body has been politicized, commodified and gentrified for external gain. The time has come for us to uproot these beliefs so that our birthright of worthiness and enoughness may arise to be claimed.

So why burlesque as medicine?

To show up and share oneself and one's own female presence and energy is a bold and needed action in today's society.

In light of thousands of years worth of conditioning, sensual female energy can feel taboo. What if you were to let your foxy light shine without hindrance or fear? One of the many gifts of burlesque is how it allows beauty to be front and center. There is inherent freedom and generosity in claiming one's beauty for all to see and behold. How can we allow ourselves to be seen like this if we don't take the initiative and show up for our bodies and our beauty? Some people are too uncomfortable with their own sensuality and its natural expression to be able to appreciate that same freedom of expression in others. Others may be too unsettled around the bare female form and its celebration to allow themselves to embrace the ripe, divine femininity that shimmies and shakes before them. If someone doesn't like burlesque, I am not here to convince anyone to love it if that love or curiosity isn't already present. I am here, however, to lovingly challenge you to expand beyond your comfort zone, either in movement or thought so that you can become comfortable with a deeper commitment to your own self-expression. When we say yes to whatever action or pursuit sparks joy in our hearts, we create the conditions for unparalleled change and the reclamation of the truth that we are both worthy and ready to connect with a deep expression of love in our hearts and our lives. More than ever, we need people to begin waking up to the innocence and inherent beauty of the female form and its full, sensual expression. As I have repeated often, we can only see in others what is already present within ourselves.

I want to add to that we can only learn through example. When one person makes the brave choice to own their joy and honor their unique voice, it acts as a giant game of dominoes. Inspiration and recognition build and resonate with each dropped and fallen thought of not-enoughness and momentum builds exponentially.

The female body and feminine energy have been disrespected, manipulated and labeled as sinful for too long. This limited view must come to an end if we are to progress as a species and heal life on our planet. Plenty of people will revolt against the change, likely the ones who have benefitted from the subjugation of women and their bodies. Love brings up everything unlike itself, and if we choose to anchor ourselves in fierce, unapologetic love, we must be prepared for those blocks, and the people who hold them, to rise up and scream out in resistance. It may be expressed as judgment, oppression or hate, but the root cause is that persistent belief in separation that desperately needs healing. Sure, not everyone will be interested in acknowledging their own pain as they're busy trolling or hurling insults, but stay steady with the knowledge that when you act from your heart, you can do no wrong. You are not responsible for anyone's reactions to what you are expressing or putting out into the world. You are responsible for your own responses and reactions. Are you willing to show up, tell your truth and receive the experience of being seen and heard in doing so? It is time to come back home to ourselves and receive the love, attention, and affirmation that we so deeply desire. No matter the stage we stand on, we have an opportunity to be seen and heard in our authentic truth and know that we are safe in doing so.

The key energy of reception is about relaxing and simply saying yes. This is the gift of feminine energy. As we cultivate a practice of receiving, let's notice how much of the lack that we experience in our lives is rooted in rejecting the gifts that surround us. One way of experiencing this is to let yourself receive compliments. Simply saying 'thank you' and letting it land in your consciousness can be a very hard task. Another way is to take in someone's joyful response to your friendly smile. Notice where you can soften in your everyday life. Where can you cultivate the willingness to receive? Therein lies the practice of feminine energy. It is simple, profound and very effective. This energy has been waiting for us since the day we were born. I invite you to begin to play by saying yes to it.

TRUTH

To me, it is far easier to strip in front of a room full of strangers than it is to get up and speak my raw truth. It is, however, an edge of discomfort that I now lean into with anticipation of greater things to come. If I am to create the conditions for change that I want to see, I have to start by reminding myself that we all stand on the shoulders of giants.

We are blessed with so many brave people who have risked their lives in order to tell their truth and stand up for what they believe in. I salute them and invite you to imagine what they risk so that the highest truth of equality can be shouted and affirmed the world over. I hope their example will make your battles easier to fight.

I want to take this element of risky truth-telling and bring it to a deeper level by paying attention to the sexual, sensual woman who has agency and the know-how to bring her work to the world. The independent, sexually liberated female energy is one that our world desperately needs and yet it is one that is consistently demeaned, belittled and stigmatized. We must correct how we see this paradigm and archetype so that we can grow more fully and honor the wild woman within whose needed voice has been silenced for too long. You don't have to be a woman to have this archetype within you. Whether or not you identify with this archetype or have any sense of its presence within you, I can guarantee that you are descended from them. We all carry their blood in our veins and it is time we honor our lineage and the presence of this energy within us.

Burlesque is comprised of these women at all levels of awakening and empowerment. No one is perfect and I acknowledge the deeply human element of my community and female-dominant communities at large. More than ever, a diversity of bodies with accompanying voices are stepping forward to be seen, heard, and celebrated. I honor every shape, color, texture, age, and identity of the women who say yes to getting out of their own way and tapping into the dance that makes their heart sing.

To confidently present one's body as art is a powerful expression of belonging and claiming one's self.

When pulled out of the halls of institutional art, the naked human body is a lightning rod for shame, comparison, judgment, and self-projection. If we have been taught to either hate or punish our bodies, it makes sense that our hair-trigger reaction to the nude human form is one of shame, hate, and wanting to hide the offensive action or form. When we see someone owning, claiming and celebrating their body, it can bring up everything within us that stands between our own acceptance and realization of love.

Loving our bodies is a potent tool for self-acceptance and self-actualization that benefits everyone with whom we come into contact.

I'm not talking about the slick leaders who have teams of stylists, content generators and marketers behind them. I'm talking about everyday people who decide enough is enough and who start to bravely live their truth and create incredible ripple effects that impact each and every one of us. We are in a time of major institutional breakdowns and re-assessments. It is a potent time to begin questioning how we can create lives of meaning, value, and purpose according to our own soul's resonance. It is radical and necessary to begin showing up in our truth, no matter how clumsy its initial expression. We cannot run until we've learned to walk.

Using the medium of the unclothed human form to connect and express is, quite simply, a radical act.

When we witness someone simply sharing what they love without trying to change or apologize for their body, magic happens. What better conduit for radical action than a mode of self-expression that challenges social belief, mores, and valuation in real-time?

Burlesque showed me that my crazy ideas had a home onstage in front of hollering crowds, but more importantly, it showed me that I had a right to my own joy. Dancing lit up every part of my heart and tapped into an aquifer of creative energy deep within me. I found belonging and for the first time felt celebrated for what came straight from my heart and through my body.

You don't have to get on stage and strip to find peace. That is how I discovered my joy, found deep belonging in my own body and a greater sense of belonging in the company of my community.

Your task is to discover what drives satisfaction in your life. We each act out our days on a stage of sorts, whether it's at work, in our families and within our communities.

Imagine stepping into a spotlight. What could you claim and express in order to step into full alignment with the joy that lights up your heart? Do you know, or are you unsure? If you know what it is, are you willing to begin? If you don't know what your outlet is, are you willing to discover it? If you're drawing a blank here, are you willing to wonder? Are you willing to keep asking the question so that you wake up or walk straight into the answer?

As Rumi so beautifully said, whatever you are seeking is seeking you. When we step into a space of wondering, we can more easily receive what's meant for us. The energetic openness of this word alone can be a beautiful balm for a wandering and wondering mind.

THE SHIFT

If we want to change ourselves, we must examine our own beliefs and programming. Anything that remains unconscious and unobserved will continue to call the shots, keeping us in patterns of behavior that will continue to produce the same disappointing results. I learned in my rebirthing training that belief is merely one thought that is thought repeatedly. When we change that thought, we can change our beliefs and move mountains in the blink of an eye.

What if you began to choose differently? What if you lived your life and made choices based upon your inherent worthiness of love? What would change? What would shift in your life? Are you willing to give yourself permission to go a little deeper and wonder what else could come into your life if you made a decision that you are here for a reason with a unique gift to deliver to the world?

For us to begin to create new possibilities and awarenesses for ourselves, I offer you the following list to explore and practice at your own speed.

1. Commit to your own worthiness
2. Tell the truth faster a.k.a. radical truth-telling
3. Clear any destructive or unsupportive beliefs around your worth and deservedness of love
4. Get clear on your relationship to God/Creator/Divinity/ higher power
5. Embrace your own free will and ability to choose
6. Commit to kindness and affirm continuously that you are still learning

None of this is required, and your willingness to move through this list has zero bearing on whether or not you're a good or bad person. You can choose to work on yourself or not – at the end of the day, what matters is how have you been treating yourself and those around you as a result. The question is, now that you know all of this, what do you choose to do?

COMMIT TO YOUR OWN WORTHINESS

Commitment is nothing more than a decision. Just like saying yes at the wedding altar or signing a contract that obligates you to partake in a collective, consensual agreement, commitment is an ironclad framing device for your own life choices. It is not without its challenges. I used to run screaming from commitment in any shape or form because it felt like a jail sentence. If I committed to doing XYZ, that meant I couldn't do A–W which pitched me into major FOMO (Fear Of Missing Out). I know I am not alone in this. Think about how many people are terrified of commitment or avoid it like the plague.

When I started performing regularly, I realized I needed to rehearse so that I could get better at my acts. I resisted the studio rental fees, the time required to do the thing and the countless costume alterations, changes, and decorations. I would get so frustrated and figure that I could just half-ass it until that thought came back and bit me in the other half of my ass that I had left offstage. I realized that if I wanted to be a great performer, I owed it to myself and my reputation to show up, rehearse and do the best act I could with everything I had. That realization and subsequent decision formed a huge commitment for me to honor and it changed my approach and creative process for the better.

As someone who used to dodge commitment, I know how scary it can feel to make such a strong decision. To choose decisively is to say no to every other possible avenue of action. That can trigger some serious fear of deprivation. The trick about this fear is that it is a self-sustaining mechanism of paralysis. If by making a decision we feel that we are somehow robbing ourselves of free will and infinite choices, we end up not making decisions which in turn keeps us stuck. By making a strong choice, we are not actually depriving ourselves of anything—far from it. By choosing a certain path or action from a place of love and self-ownership, we nourish our goals and provide crucial framing for ourselves to plug deeply into our own fulfillment. There is no deprivation in commitment to self. If anything, it's like hitting the jackpot.

All of this in mind, are you willing to commit to the truth that you are worthy of love and deserve everything that you dream of? Notice if there is a "no" present. What is your greatest fear about accepting that you are worthy? What is scary about accepting the truth that you are enough as you are? When we shine the light of our consciousness into these murky shadows of half-truths and defense mechanisms, we can dissipate the fear as we step into deeper acceptance of our inherent worthiness.

Try it—find a mirror and tell yourself that you are worthy of everything you desire. Notice your response. Share with yourself your greatest fears about saying yes or no to whatever you are negotiating at that moment. Repeat this exercise until it begins to take hold.

TELLING THE TRUTH FASTER, A.K.A. RADICAL TRUTH-TELLING

How would your life change if you told the truth all the time? What would happen if you told the truth in your work, family, friends, and intimate relationships? Is your first thought that everything would explode into flames? Would you be left in the dust to wallow in your unworthiness all alone? Or would you finally be able to step out from the weight of expectations, frustrations, judgments, and your false sense of "not-enoughness?"

Telling myself the truth was one of the hardest things I've ever done. Admitting that I was starving myself into a serious illness was one of them. Another one was that I deserved to be backstage with burlesque rockstars even though sometimes I wanted to crumple up into a corner and hide from my own feelings of being a worthless fraud.

Now when I look at myself in the mirror, I tell the truth. I see what the years have brought me and I see the traces of what my many life choices have left on my face and body. Instead of doubling down on self-doubt or self-hate, I follow it up with "and I love myself" BECAUSE THAT IS THE TRUTH!

Stepping into deeper ownership of my own self-love was a game-changer because it forced me to stay closely aligned with the truth of who I am. I couldn't flake off into "self-hate town" anymore. If I was teaching and preaching this to other people and supporting friends who were moving through hard times with their own bodies, how could I leave myself out of that equation? How could I be a part of this truth if I have excluded myself from that consciousness?

My truth is that I am here to promote love so that we can all come home to our own hearts. How could I teach that and simultaneously harbor any personal lies that have long outlived their purpose? My commitment to helping others heal made me tell the truth and reap the benefits of this courageous action.

Telling the truth is a vibrant form of love. It may not feel like love if truth involves fury or anger toward another person, but I assure you that truth resides in the heart. You might start telling radical truth and discover that you hold anger toward another person. This anger might trigger fantasies of you telling everyone what you think about them with guns blazing and no one left standing. If something like this comes up for you, I ask you to look beneath the revenge fantasies. Where are you not holding yourself in love? Where in your past relationships have you bitten your tongue so that your true feelings remain obscured? What are you protecting by doing so? Can you see how refusing to tell the truth is preventing you from fully allowing the energy of love to be present in your life?

I saw a greeting card once that said all relationships are either a blessing or a lesson. I would argue that they're both. I remember thinking about how certain relationships have a certain amount of pain or struggle inherent in them. If we attract a partner who serves a perfect purpose for a short period of time, that relationship will conclude eventually. The question is, do we prolong that eventuality out of a desire to avoid sadness or conflict? As a result, have we actually put ourselves through more suffering? If certain relationships are to contain a certain amount of growth and discomfort, isn't it more efficient to tell the truth faster when things aren't working so as to access the easier, clearer path sooner?

GETTING CLEAR ON & HEALING THE RELATIONSHIP WITH GOD/ DIVINE/UNIVERSE/HIGHER POWER

When I began my breathwork training in 2009, I came face-to-face with the fact that I was really, really mad at "God." I put that word in quotes because, as Eckhart Tolle put it so beautifully in his book "*The Power of Now*," the word God has become empty of meaning through thousands of years of misuse. There has been so much harm, trauma, oppression and violence done in the name of God and Jesus Christ that it is understandable for people to have a knee-jerk reaction to the words we use to refer to them. Many have weaponized those names and used them in ways that both demonstrate their own personal lack of understanding of the Divine as they promote the opposite of love and acceptance.

Sondra Ray, a pioneer and the mother of rebirthing breathwork says that our relationship with God affects all of our relationships in our lives. God/Universe, etcetera is Source Energy—it is the animating force of life that gives shape to our human landscape. We develop our beliefs and connections to a higher power through our family/home environment, education and sometimes personal revelation. When the people who are meant to teach us, tell us that God is mean, cruel, or loves conditionally, that becomes our definition. Our parents, our communities, our cultures all have different ways of teaching us by example, and if their words and actions imply that God doesn't love everyone equally, we fall into the myth of separation.

So how do we heal this God wound? How do we come into intimate contact with Source energy and make peace with it?

The first step is to cultivate willingness. If there is no desire to heal this primary relationship, or a strong attachment to the pain or trauma that keeps the individual locked into separation, then one won't get very far. Willingness may not swing the doors of forgiveness wide open, but it will undo the latch and maybe even nudge the door gently open. Willingness is seed desire. When we can say yes to being willing, our road opens up before us.

PLAYING WITH NEW THOUGHTS

Many espouse the power of affirmations, myself included, yet sometimes they can feel inaccessible. If this is the case for you, try beginning the affirmation with the phrase, "I am willing to ..." and notice what shifts.

I now choose to make peace with God/Universe/Higher Power as He/She/It/this force has my highest good in mind always.

I now open my mind and heart to what God may be.

I accept that love is always with me and that I am loved unconditionally.

If that feels like too much, try beginning the affirmation with:

I am willing to ...

I am ready to …

Take a moment to write your own affirmation here and begin with, "I am willing to…" Sit with it and notice how it lands. Keep playing until you find an affirmation that vibrates deeply with your sense of wellbeing.

The second step is to affirm that source energy/God/Goddess/ Universe is on your side no matter what. This may feel like an odd thought to think if you believe God is a force to be feared and a source of separation and inequality. These things are not God, they represent the ways flawed humans have used the concept of God against one another.

Start with noticing. Begin to notice how source energy is infused in everything you come into contact with. Allow yourself to notice the beauty in your days, especially from nature. Sunlight on trees, the wind that blows and animates, the delicate color and presence of a beautiful flower or plant, or a chance encounter with an animal either wild or domesticated. This all-pervasive energy of love is all around us, always. Allow yourself to recognize the beauty and alignment that surrounds you, even if you are feeling profoundly misaligned or if you have acted in a way that doesn't feel supportive or loving toward yourself or those close to you.

God is the great YES, the master affirmative in our universe. If you believe something to be true, the universe will say yes to it. Many spiritual and holy texts remind us that our word is our bond. Words have a powerful and profound impact on how we experience and perceive life. If we affirm that life is hard or that we are too ugly to be considered lovable, the universe will say yes to that and support us in creating a reality based on those words. Belief is simply one thought, thought repeatedly. If we change the seed thought that results in unhelpful, limiting or even destructive beliefs, we can literally create a new life for ourselves.

There are many systems and institutions that bank on us continuing to believe that God is a punitive, masculine, dominant force. Notice how the patriarchal systems of governance and rule have made God in their image. But also realize we have to access history books and deep, cultural rituals that suggest God is considered a feminine force. The destructive systems at play in our world benefit greatly from using God as a righteous authority that justifies their harmful actions. Although we may not be able to topple those forces by sheer might alone, we can make the quiet, inner shift that allows us to access the mystery of God/Universe/Anima and slowly pull back any support either conscious or unconscious from systems that perpetuate a misaligned version of source energy.

EMBRACE FREE WILL

> *"Everything can be taken from a man but one thing: the last of the human freedoms—to choose one's attitude in any given set of circumstances, to choose one's own way."*
>
> —Viktor E. Frankl, *Man's Search for Meaning*

In every moment, we have a choice. We hold an innate ability to make choices according to our own free will. If you are someone who has been taught that your choices are somehow wrong or shameful, I invite you to pull back out of that thought and notice two things. One, was your thought or choice based on free will? Was it something that supported your life and life in general? Two, was that thought or choice perceived as some kind of threat to those who condemned it? As you get comfortable with these questions and the answers they bring up, know that other people may view your powerful choosing as scary. Usually, this is how people react when they have some stake in you staying fixed in the same old choices and decisions.

An example of this rising "threat" of free will is how the weight loss industry is responding to the body positivity movement. This sweeping social movement states that there is no wrong way to have a body and that we can all be healthy no matter what size our body is. Health At Every Size (haescommunity.com) is a wonderful online resource that works to end weight discrimination by educating about size acceptance and challenging myths about weight and worth. Companies like Weight Watchers are trying to co-opt the movement by folding body positivity and inclusivity into their marketing. As a business, they perceive a threat to their bottom line which has, in turn, spawned a marketing makeover. Let's be clear here—any business model rooted in weight loss for profit is not body positive. Your weight has nothing to do with your worth or who you are. This liberating truth is a deep threat to the diet industry and any industry that makes money off of women who feel they need to change how they look to please others. Let's be clear here though—the only threat is to profit margins, not human life.

When I speak of threat here, I am talking about the perceived threat. I am not talking about an actual physical or emotional threat that endangers others. If violence is in the seed thought within you, get thee to a therapist, anger management training or easier yet, the section in this book on forgiveness.

Anger is not justifiable. When we engage in harmful activities, we set ourselves back from making progress and accepting that healing is possible.

If you find that you have a build-up of physical fury or rage, you need to start moving your body in order to release that energy in a constructive way. From any kind of dance and martial arts to Tai Chi, Wu Tao or Qi Gong, there are many ways to tap into and access your physical energy to help release pent-up feelings.

One more note on anger—it is considered a secondary emotion, meaning it is the result of another feeling, usually grief, fear or sadness. It is fully possible for you to dive beneath the waves of anger to see the root cause of your strong feelings. It is also fully possible for you to be able to nurture and resolve those feelings in order to access the deeper levels of your own possibilities. You have one wild and precious life. Please use as little as possible of it on anger.

When we say yes to our own ability to freely choose how we respond to situations, a world of possibility opens up. This infinite field of possibility allows us to actively say yes to what is supportive, nourishing and life-affirming. When we comfortably reside in our birthright of free will, we powerfully affect our own lives for the better, learning curves and all.

COMMIT TO KINDNESS & AFFIRM THAT YOU ARE STILL LEARNING

When we commit to kindness as a way to navigate the world, we create softness and safety wherever we go. Some of the most unexpectedly moving moments I've experienced were when I smiled or offered kindness to someone who was looking exceptionally grumpy or put out. As a native New Yorker, I have had the opportunity to practice kindness with many people from all walks of life—from homeless people, screaming children, their stressed moms, loud high schoolers, older people, or CEOs in suits. It moves me to see the softening in others that comes from my own softening.

For you commitment-phobes out there, rest easy with the word. Commitment is simply a decision. If you are willing to practice kindness, make that choice and let yourself bring it into every corner of your life.

What might this look like? Take a moment and ask yourself, what would it look like if I were to commit to kindness. Sit with this for a moment and notice what comes up. Do you notice any new possibilities emerging in your relationships, or how you treat yourself day in and day out? Stay with this thought and play with it. When we can make a solid choice rooted in kindness, we are the ones who benefit the most.

Kindness is friendly, generous and considerate. Who doesn't want to feel that all the time? If you are someone who is kind to others but not very kind to yourself, I want to offer you the possibility of stepping into radical kindness. What does this look like? It means being friendly, generous and considerate to yourself. If you are navigating a challenging situation or needing to have a hard conversation with someone, I lovingly dare you to put yourself first in the interaction. Offer, do and create things that feel kind TO YOU. When we come from our hearts, we can do no wrong. When you are kind to yourself, you are ultimately kind to everyone.

You are the motherboard as it were, so begin with you and watch what happens …

One last thought here—each and every one of us are still learning. Life is practice and the learning curves don't quit. As a recovering perfectionist, I found that repeating the affirmation "I am still learning" was a powerful panacea for the self-inflicted anger and punishment I was accustomed to piling on myself. When we choose to affirm that we are on life's grand learning curve, it puts things into perspective. It offers an opportunity to acknowledge where you are and what you are doing free of judgment or expectation. I find this phrase to be a wonderful demonstration of kindness to myself and anyone I encounter.

YOU AND YOUR BODY ARE INNOCENT

Newsflash—by being in a body no matter its gender, you are innocent. In the eyes of love, there is no guilt or shame associated with having a body. Whoever may argue differently is someone whose view of life and their own body is limited. You can love them by wishing them well on their own journey to truth. If you have been taught that there is an inherent guilt or expectation connected to the body you were born into, I invite you to make a radical commitment to your own innocence. This is how you can begin to weed out limiting thoughts that are rooted in shame, guilt, fear or judgment.

When we embrace our innocence, we free up our anchors to the past. This was a term I learned when I was in my breathwork training. It initially struck me as overly simple only later to reveal itself as a powerful form of medicine. What do the words 'guilt' and 'shame' mean to you? How does your body feel when you read those words? If you notice a sense of recoil or heaviness enter, this passage is for you.

When we clear our relationships with ourselves, and especially our relationships with our bodies, we can more fully show up within our lives and create the conditions to receive the realization of our goals.

Undressing the Truth

What is your greatest fear about life? If it came true, what would happen?

Who are you proving right by staying small? To whom do you owe this unconscious loyalty?

And if you dropped your fears, shame, indiscretions, or guilt … Who would you be? What would you do, free from that burden?

Walk with the question—how can I love myself today?

Begin to harness the following affirmations:

I now notice the truth when it is present and I take in and respond according to the highest good of the situation.

I do what I can with what I have. My being and presence are enough.

DEEPER TOOLS: FACING THE APOCALYPSE WITH A FULL HEART

"Until one is committed, there is hesitancy, the chance to draw back, always ineffectiveness. Concerning all acts of initiative and creation, there is one elementary truth the ignorance of which kills countless ideas and splendid plans: that the moment one definitely commits oneself, then providence moves too.

All sorts of things occur to help one that would never otherwise have occurred. A whole stream of events issues from the decision, raising in one's favor all manner of unforeseen incidents, meetings and material assistance which no man could have dreamed would have come his way.

Whatever you can do or dream you can, begin it. Boldness has genius, power, and magic in it. Begin it now."

—William Hutchison Murray

Fun fact—the word apocalypse comes from the Greek word "to uncover." The folks who proclaim the world is ending are simply foretelling the end of great illusions, lies, and limited thinking. I don't know what it will take for everyone on this planet to surrender to love. The conditions of intolerance, cruelty, and oppression are increasing in volume and density. Let us always remember the love in our hearts and bodies when confronted with fear of any form and speak its truth. If Divine Truth were to rise and dismantle all the systems rooted in inequality and separation, who would each of us be? Does the uncertainty of that scenario bring you agita or concern? If it does, what if you were willing to trust that love is present and that you are on your own perfect soul path? How does holding that thought change the outcome?

Should our world or lives end tomorrow, will you have created or done whatever it is that you want to do? To paraphrase the brilliant poet, Mary Oliver, "What will you do with this one wild and precious life?"

What are your most deeply held dreams and beliefs? Notice the first thing that comes up. What stands in between you and it? What will it take to get you out of your own way so that you can access those dreams and turn them into reality? So you know, I'm writing this for myself as much as I am for you, dear reader.

Where are you saying no to love in your life? Where in your life are you unwilling to receive love? This can manifest in a variety of ways, and if you're not sure, check what your relationships are to food, sex, and money. These three things comprise how we both give and receive energy. How easy is it for you to give? How easy is it for you to receive?

It's time for us to practice discernment and compassion. We only ever have the here and now. Yesterday is done and tomorrow doesn't exist yet. What is it that you choose to do with this gift of now? Whatever it may be, I invite you to welcome the energy and presence of love into every corner of your mind and body so that you can set yourself up exceptionally well so you can create the life that you want to lead.

I realize this is a rather grand statement, but my intention here is to plant the seeds of a radically different and profoundly new way of looking at your life.

Are you willing to live from a place of love, allowing your heart to call the shots? What if you shifted how you define your meaning, value, and purpose from one based on external identifiers (job, income, looks, etc.) into a place of total self-ownership reliant upon only your inner sense of connection and love of yourself? Looking at your life this way may feel risky. It definitely involves overturning personal beliefs and challenging old perceptions. That may feel scary, but it is necessary to create the change you seek. I welcome this new way of thinking for you because love awaits you on each step of this brave journey.

I dedicate this chapter to four of the modern godmothers of neo-burlesque—Imogen Kelly, Indigo Blue, World Famous *BOB* and Bonnie Dunn.

Imogen Kelly is an Australian neo-burlesque star who has revolutionized striptease laws and made a hell of a career for herself. She is a wonder of grace and beauty. She played a big role in changing Australia's laws and attitudes about stripping. She has shared very generously about surviving breast cancer with a double mastectomy and not letting that stop her from getting onstage. Imogen is a gift and I am so grateful to her.

Indigo Blue is the Headmistress of the Academy of Burlesque in Seattle, WA and the founder of BurlyCon, the world's only burlesque educational convention. Indigo's wit, charm, and talent make her a delightful performer to watch, but her dedicated work in social activism and erotic education make her a major foundational player in the global neo-burlesque scene. I also happen to adore her.

World Famous *BOB* is a legend in the burlesque and drag worlds. Having overcome an extremely hard early life, *BOB* created her life her way and learned how better to love herself every step of the way. She is also an unwavering beam of love and service to the burlesque legends who paved the way for us all to have the careers and stage lives that we do. She taught me that loving fiercely is a powerful way to show people that they are seen and also accountable for their actions. She has had a powerful impact on my life and I love her forever for it.

Bonnie Dunn was a godmother of burlesque in New York City. She was originally from New Orleans and brought a sexy, raunchy and fabulous style to the scene in NYC. She ran Le Scandal, the longest running burlesque show in NYC, and was a kind, loving, gentle and hilarious person and performer. Thanks to Bonnie's dedication to giving neo-burlesque a home and many stages, the NYC burlesque world is all the richer for her legacy, employment, and commitment to us all. I miss her terribly and am grateful to have known and loved her. Please google her to catch a glimpse of this delightful woman.

Making Peace with the Body

What we experience and perceive in life boils down to the relationship we have with ourselves. We are here to change and grow. We are here to learn that we are love, pure and simple. As we expand into the emerging consciousness of oneness, we each play a crucial role in our own and each other's awakening. Life is here to reveal us to ourselves. When we plant the seed of loving intention with each choice we make, we can create a seismic shift in our own and each other's lives. Do not underestimate your power! As we peel away the falsehoods and the programming that tell us we are somehow not enough, we get a chance to expand into what has been waiting for us this whole time—our truth and our work in this lifetime.

Some people will cling to the fading, old paradigm as if their life depends on it. These are the same folks who will resist the rising awareness and accessibility of love. Just as we are loveable in our truth, they too are lovable in their negotiation. Change can feel really scary and be very destabilizing. It can also bring up a lot of challenging thoughts and feelings. No matter how big the changes in our lives, if we can return to love and reassure ourselves that we have our own backs, the tides of change turn into a proactive push toward where we need to be and what we each need to be doing. Trust in ourselves is vital. This doesn't mean we have to have all the answers - far from it. When we form the intention to trust ourselves no matter what's going on in our lives, we begin to create a powerful resonance of self-reliance and resilience. If there is any part of ourselves that is not ready to assume the mantle of deep self-love and trust or the faith that it is even possible, there is work still to be done.

This work is a gift and if any of these words are making you think "Oh Jeez, back to school I go…" I want to offer you this knowledge: you are farther along than you think you are. Not only that, you are exactly where you need to be in order to be having this experience.

I am writing these words from my own emerging place of unity. It is my intention to promote and provoke the same in you. These pages hold the trace of love expressed through my words that are intended to reach your heart as they reach your mind and eyes. I am just as much on this path as you are and am navigating my own learning curves as I grow and expand my awareness and connection to life. My intention is to share my process so as to lift the worry, fear, shame and/or judgment that you and others may hold about this sacred journey back to the self.

If you are someone whose body image has played a powerful role in your learning experience in this life, welcome to the party. I'm glad you're here.

The body is the way and the tool through which we perceive and experience life. No matter what our relationship is to it, our bodies are our learning devices in this lifetime. As a woman, I have had to unlearn what society holds dear and precious in order to discover a profound sense of love and appreciation for myself.

From my starved early years, I am so grateful to know that gaining weight is not a death knell of my worthiness. Neither is getting older. I'm still me, and that is f**king fabulous.

When we can get out of our own way and choose to stop being affected by how others perceive us and claim our deep worth and lovability, we experience lasting change. Boy is that easier said than done, but you know what? It's possible and happens when you are ready to accept it. There is no rush, no ticking clock on the way back home to our sacred center of self. There is no alarm bell waiting to ring because you somehow aren't enough or where you need to be by a certain time. This journey is a privilege that can take a lifetime to fully integrate. What matters is that you're on the path and present with whatever you are negotiating in each moment. What doesn't matter is how far along the path you are. What also doesn't matter, is where you are in comparison to anyone else.

Accepting our own bodies is a gargantuan feat for anyone who has ever felt poorly about themselves. The richness that lies within is waiting for us to wake up to it.

It is patient, has been there forever, and is endless.

Some call this the still, small center of self, others call it a spark of God, or the core of consciousness. As we peel back the layers of limitation, we get to uncover, discover and create a life where we can choose to love and radically accept our bodies as they are. When we make that decision, we create a safe container of self where nothing can enter without our permission. We can more easily neutralize any charge that may trigger us back into limited thinking because we have replaced that deficit with love and a deeper acknowledgment of our spirit.

We are here to love and be loved, period.

Our bodies matter and are loveable, but ultimately they are a means to an end. A body is just a device that allows us to deliver our riches to the world.

When we make a choice to love ourselves, we create an experiential anchor in joy. If this connection to the heart is a newer relationship for you, I invite you to begin to notice what happens around you when you decide to live from your heart. When we consciously embark on a path, trip or quest wherein we are led by our hearts, we give permission for the great mystery to enter and work its magic.

When we make space for love, it affords us unlimited space to feel, to experience, and to inhabit the present moment with engagement and connection.

So how do we get there? How do we begin to allow these deeper awarenesses and embark on the most fulfilling journey of our lives? We begin as we would with any journey, with a single step followed by another, followed by another, and so on.

What follows here is a series of exercises and tools for you to use sequentially or at random. The goal here is to foster deeper self-awareness and to acknowledge which part of your belief systems are not in alignment with the energy of love. If you are someone who treats yourself a bit roughly as you learn new things, please know that there is no expectation and no ticking clock here. This is the most valuable journey you will ever take, and if it takes you a week or a year or a lifetime, so be it. We all have our own rhythm and pace and what matters is that we are on the path, not how far along we are. There is no good, bad, right or wrong as we practice being ourselves in a more authentic way.

There is just learning, and love.

HEAL YOUR TRAUMA

If someone has experienced trauma, the memory is stored in the body. The trauma in our body has the ability to override logical, rational thinking in favor of keeping us safe and far away from a repeat trauma, sometimes at steep costs. In his brilliant essay "White Supremacy as a Trauma Response" on Salon.com, author and therapist Resmaa Menakem explains:

"Contrary to what many people believe, trauma is not primarily an emotional response. *Trauma always happens in the body. It is a spontaneous protective mechanism used by the body to stop or thwart further (or future) potential damage.* Trauma is not a flaw or a weakness. It is a highly effective tool for safety and survival. Trauma is also not an event. Trauma is the body's protective response to an event—or a series of events—that it perceives as potentially dangerous. An embedded trauma response can manifest as fighting, fleeing, or freezing— or as some combination of constriction, pain, fear, dread, anxiety, unpleasant (and/or sometimes pleasant) thoughts, reactive behaviors, or other sensations and experiences. *This trauma then gets stuck in the body—and stays stuck there until it is addressed.* Our rational brain can't stop it from occurring, and it can't talk our body out of it."

We cannot change what has happened to us in the past, but we can choose to nurture, heal and resolve our wounds so that we set ourselves up well for whatever life brings us in the future. If you have suffered a trauma, please get help for it so that you can heal your body and your mind. More than ever, there are therapists who are gifted at working with folks who have suffered trauma and have PTSD. There are affordable clinics in most big cities. The internet is full of resources for you to discover the way home through healing your trauma. I realize this is much easier said than done, but what matters is that you begin. It doesn't matter if it takes a year, a decade, or the rest of your life to work through what happened. What matters is that you're showing up for yourself and claiming the fact that YOU ARE WORTH HEALING! If any voice inside or outside of your head tells you otherwise, know that those voices are anchored and invested in maintaining your trauma status quo because deep down there is a payoff, and that payoff is often that of remaining a victim.

Enough is enough. You can do this. The rest of your life and the whole world is waiting for you and supporting you in your healing process.

DETHRONING THE EGO

Oh, ego. The root of this word is the Latin word that means "I am." According to *A Course in Miracles*, the ego is what we create when we have the thought that we are separate from God. If ACIM isn't your bag, another way of putting it is that the ego is the false self, the bottomless pit that holds the seeds of the seven deadly sins according to Christianity. The ego says, "me before anyone else" and it is responsible for the pain we hold on this planet.

I feel strongly that burlesque is love, but the people who dance, shimmy and shake are all human. Whereas burlesque is beauty and artistry, the egos of some dancers can wreck a relationship, dressing room, company, venue or entire scene with stunning speed. Ego-driven show business shenanigans may make for great gossip, but it is immensely destructive. We all have egos. We all would do well to keep them in check. The ego is the result of a belief in separation. Why would anyone squash, connive, sabotage, or feel threatened by the beauty and art of another if they themselves knew that love is of and with them always? When the ego acts up, it is because there is a form of starvation or deprivation present that makes the person feel as if it's them against the world.

It's not you against the world and it never has been.

Even if your lived and learned experience has taught you that life is a struggle or that you don't deserve love, or that you are somehow bad or guilty for simply being, take a deep breath and blow that sh*t away. None of this is true. We are love and we are light and we are here to heal. Yes, we create and participate in complex structures and relationships, but at the end of the day, we are here to learn how to love.

I believe our ego to be our vessel in this life. Without it, we would be diffuse energy without personality. The ego does bear some gifts, but they are not ones to identify with lest they be taken away. There is such a thing as a healthy ego, such as standing up for yourself, asking for what you want and owning your gifts. When the egoic behaviors begin to tip the scales and enter Godzilla territory, then there is an opportunity to cultivate awareness and begin to plant seeds of change.

If ego is an issue for you, or if you have been told that your ego is a problem, and you wish to change, take a moment and write down all that your ego holds to be true.

If you're not sure or can't come up with anything, envision your ego sitting across the table from you and ask it directly, writing down its responses. Its whole function is to protect you because you didn't learn early on that you are always connected to Source Energy and thus never in a state of lack. You have never been lacking in love even if you were shown otherwise. Please begin to walk in the shoes and with the mindset of love as you navigate this terrain of change. You are not only safe to do this, but you are also offering yourself the opportunity to level up and evolve into a higher state of consciousness.

Our ego can be our friend, but please remove it from the position of CEO in your life. Your loving heart is more than equipped to pick up that mantle. Begin to play, expand, and learn with this.

DISMANTLING MISOGYNY

How much time, energy and money do we pour into how we look? How much of that is rooted in lack, as in "I'm not enough just as I am?"

How much do we rely on what is external to define what is internal? I will never forget when the WonderBra first came out and women rushed in droves to buy them. I remember speaking to a friend about them (I believe she owned a few of these bras) and thinking to myself, what happens if you get a guy and then take your bra off in front of him? Isn't that false advertising? Mind you, I was pretty young when I was considering this and hadn't yet realized how much fun these external attributes can be to play dress-up with and how much partners may enjoy the enhancements. My friend replied, "Oh, I leave it on. My boobs look horrible without it." I was gobsmacked. She was gorgeous and super fortunate to have a very attractive body. For whatever reason, she couldn't see it. She grew annoyed when I objected to her characterization of her self. I didn't see an ugly woman—I saw my beautiful friend who was lucky enough to have a date on Saturday night. After we reached an impasse and she changed the subject, I couldn't help but feel that something was really wrong here.

I have nothing against makeup, shapewear, plastic surgery, wigs, eyelash extensions, etc. if they make a woman feel beautiful. Where I begin to see red flags is when women feel that they are dependent upon these enhancements. I am concerned about women who, when deprived of these enhancements or not able to maintain a certain look, start to believe they are somehow horrible people who don't deserve love or affection. This may sound dramatic but I have seen it everywhere over the course of my life. We live in a highly visual culture, and a capitalistic one at that. If a woman is either unattractive or unwilling to make herself pretty in order to be palatable to the general public, there is a kind of disgust or rejection that comes along with it.

Sadly, much of the time that judgment doesn't come from men but from other women. The women who first teach us this kind of misogyny are frequently our mothers who, for whatever reason, were never shown that they were more than enough and completely beautiful no matter what they looked like. This self-rejection and, at an extreme, self-hate is how we put and keep ourselves down. Our own internalized misogyny as women keeps us locked in cycles of judgment, condemnation, and jealousy against other women.

How utterly convenient this is for those in power who profit off of our distraction.

We are facing dire threats to our planet right now. How easy it is to be distracted by how our skin looks or what our dress size is. If we set down our vanity or need to "improve" how we look, we are faced with pressing, intense realities that do indeed require our attention.

The forces of distraction and suppression at the hands of big business, big pharma, partisan government and the ultra-rich (which includes religious institutions) are benefitting exceptionally well from our own feelings of "not-enoughness." If we as women were to all step into our power and agency, the powers that be wouldn't last much longer than a candle in the wind.

The suppression of autonomous choice, power, and agency over a woman's own body and its expression can end now, but only if you choose for it to be so. The action to make this happen on a universal scale boils down to the actions of each and every one of us. We cannot change what's in our world until we change ourselves.

Know that misogyny is rooted in oppression and limitation. It exists because of the patriarchal belief system that dominates and dismantles anything that stands in its way, including the essential wisdom and presence of women. To hate a woman because of who she is is to hate yourself, period. We can only do unto others as we do unto ourselves.

Does a certain kind or type of woman drive you nuts? When you bring her to mind or run into her on the street, begin with the thought "the Divine in me sees the Divine in you." When navigating tough situations, it's always wonderful to invoke Divine presence and intelligence. Notice her beauty even if it is disguised under irritating behavior or years of self-hate. Notice her fullness, gifts, and uniqueness. If you are aware of judgment, ask yourself what she represents for you. If she has had any history of tragedy, tough treatment, abuse, violation, or cruelty at the hands of her family or people close to her and has allowed what they did to her to become part of her identity and who she is, can you take a breath for her and know that she is more than what life has done to her? Please do both of you a favor and begin to see her essence, the spark that lights up her heart and her being. Pay attention to her innate beauty and individuality. If you begin to see more than just what is on the surface, you're on to something divine.

If this exercise is a struggle and she is someone you just don't like, you are welcome to release her to her highest good elsewhere. You're not doing this for others—you're doing this for you. The more we can recognize the light in other women, the more we can perceive our own. When we shift how we treat others, we automatically shift how we treat ourselves. Instead of landing in limitation (e.g. judgment, resentment, sabotage, etc), we can begin to dwell on the possibility of recognizing our own worth and deep deservedness of love.

DECOLONIZING THE BODY

In order to take apart the structures that no longer fit, we must look at the inheritance of those structures in our behaviors and how they have influenced the way we navigate life. Even if we do not come from indigenous heritage or culture, we each have indigenous land, the homeland that is each of our bodies, given to us by a line of ancestors whose names we won't ever fully know. This maiden land of ours, of our body, holds the stories and the keys to unlocking our own freedom.

If we or our forebearers benefitted from any form of oppression either inherited or present-day, we have a powerful opportunity to make amends and proactively subvert that damage by uprooting the thoughts that historically have created harmful outcomes. Decolonization is one of the ways we can liberate ourselves and the painful heritage of power or people who acted as if they were better than others. Love is not historically a part of this picture, but we can change that. With our focused intention, we can perform deep extraction of these harmful legacies so that we leave the responsibility and debt at the feet of the people who created it.

I invite you to look at your ancestry. If you are unaware of your ancestry, I invite you to dig into your own history by accessing public records and pursuing any clues or stories that you are aware of. Where were your ancestors from? What were their cultural or religious traditions? Were they allowed to practice their faith and live their lives without interference? Were any of your ancestors colonizers? Did they partake in the benefits of colonization? Were any of them in the military? Did any of them enforce oppressive or martial law upon people in a foreign land? Or were any of them complacent in the oppression, enslavement or destruction of other people or culture? Who were they? What were their stories? Notice them. Write them down. Know that you can heal this history if you choose to do so. It starts with a curious reckoning.

Just as rivers are born of snow and rain, we are made up of what our ancestors have passed along to us. Sometimes we are well aware of their guiding philosophies and life pursuits, but sometimes that inheritance is murky. We are all here to follow our own unique soul curriculum with conditions perfect for our learning and evolution. I believe we each have our own path to walk in our own way. As painful as some of the reckonings are, they are here to guide us back to love. If our ancestors created situations that still affect you today, do your part to dismantle those situations with love. If we have wronged someone or an entire community, ask for forgiveness, and forgive yourself. This work can feel quite painful, but it is necessary work if we are to lighten our loads both karmically and socially.

One possible side effect of noticing where pain lies in our histories is increased sensitivity. I pray for everyone to wake up to walking with sensitivity as we negotiate our own lives and expressions while healing our wounded world and our own histories. Sensitivity is a value to be embraced and cultivated, not squashed. When we allow ourselves to become sensitive, we can more readily hear where the pain lies, or where there is unresolved emotion in a person.

The burlesque world, like other communities, has had its fair share of controversy, uproar, and reckoning around cultural appropriation. Some people are willing to adjust and change their acts so they respect the roots of their inspiration instead of exploiting them. Others have no problem slapping some rhinestones on their glamorized fetishism and/or racism. This applies to:

- Orientalism, like geishas or concubines
- Native American tribal headdresses or ceremonial costumes
- Blackface or any appropriation of African-American and Black culture
- Specific tribal or cultural signifiers or ceremonial wear that do not lie in your own ancestral lines

- Anything that comes from a people or culture that has been suppressed, oppressed or subverted in order to financially benefit the elite few over the many

The cultures I allude to were neither respected nor honored as colonizers tore them apart and plundered their riches. We must practice vigilance when approaching themes or styles from another culture that we wish to make our own. This bloody, tragic, repetitive history has yet to be fully resolved. More than ever, we have the power and the possibility to dismantle this harmful legacy so we can give way to equity, reparations, and forgiveness.

This will be messy, uncomfortable and possibly upsetting. Your descendants and our world will thank you for it. This is necessary and good, hard work and I salute those who choose to undertake this excavation of self and history.

A note to my white readers: if you want to be the change you want to see in the world, please study and learn about anti-racism. The white supremacy that is terrorizing our country and world must come to an end, and the only way we can do that is to divest ourselves from its tentacular clutches. Become vigilant when you notice judgment rising about a brown, black, or foreign person with unique customs and traditions. Become fearless. Reach down into the roots of racist thought. Pull them up and throw them into the fire of change.

We can no longer afford to remain complacent in the face of terrorism perpetuated against our human brothers and sisters based on the color of their skin. I urge you to educate yourself because the world desperately needs us to wake up if we are to plant lasting seeds of love and possibility into the fertile earth of the present moment. Just because something is uncomfortable does not mean it is a bad thing. They don't call them growing pains for nothing. It's okay to fall down, or to learn hard lessons. "Life's purpose is to reveal us to us" as my marvelous teacher Ron Baker so often says, so what are you so scared of seeing within yourself? We are here to learn how to love and to grow toward it. I encourage you to bring your fear, your shame and your judgment along with you and to educate the parts of you that feel threatened by going into this tender, volatile territory. Do not expect anyone to educate you. This is a path we walk together, by ourselves, and yes, it is very much worth it if we give way to a stronger, louder, more established presence of love in our families, communities, countries, and world.

An Invitation

I want you to take a moment here, and breathe into your body. As you inhale, feel the path that your breath takes into your body. Notice how it feels to exhale. Observe your body. Is there anything you can relax, or unclench? Take a deep, relaxing breath.

Bring yourself into a position that is as comfortable as possible in this present moment. Once you're there, take another deep breath and allow every part of you to receive your breath. Breathing into and past your lungs, allowing your breath to steep into every cell in your body. Breathing in, say yes to your breath. Offer your body a big yes for being here and now simply by inhabiting this moment with your inhale and exhale. Sit quietly for another few breaths. Notice how you feel now. Welcome to this present moment. As you read these words, know that love is here and now. I can feel it pumping throughout my whole body as I write these words and I invite you into the vitality of it. You are always welcome in the seat of your own heart. In fact, it has been waiting for you to come home for a long time now. Allow yourself to rest here, and notice what shifts as a result.

If love is something that feels foreign or distant, I invite you to read the following passage aloud.

Today love is with me. Love is me. I am love. I communicate love. I breathe love. I eat with love. I move with love. I choose with love. I love myself. I love others. I love my body.

I am grateful for any thoughts that are not love, for they are showing me the way home.

I invite you to begin and end your day with this affirmation. When we remind ourselves of our birthright of love, it reminds us of our eternal nature and helps us defuse the incidental, temporary conflicts or interruptions we may be experiencing.

Affirmations:

I have my body for a reason, and I am now willing to accept it and myself with love. I am willing to say yes to this present moment simply by breathing in and out. I say yes to being here now, to feeling everything that is present for me at this moment, and know that I am safe. I give myself permission to identify the fullness of my feelings in this present moment and to make space for love and trust that I am safe to do so.

I now choose to feel my body by breathing into it. I expand my awareness into every inch of this beautiful body and extend the energy of love into the places that aren't yet ready to receive this new level of being. As long as I come from my heart, I can do no wrong. As long as I act from a center of love, of and for others, but primarily for myself, I trust that no matter how choppy the waters or rough the ride, I will arrive ultimately unscathed and instead purified by the energy of love, that divine fire that burns away mistruth, and illusion.

Stripping Down to Core Truths

What would happen if you were to wake up in this moment and choose to make peace with your body? Are you willing to perceive your body as a sacred vessel for lived experience, the playing field of this game of life? Take a moment and notice how this makes you feel.

Closing Thoughts

The journey through life is an unexpected one paved with trials, travails, and rewards. In his seminal work "The Hero With A Thousand Faces," cultural anthropologist Joseph Campbell says:

"The agony of breaking through personal limitations is the agony of spiritual growth. Art, literature, myth and cult, philosophy, and ascetic disciplines are instruments to help the individual past his limiting horizons into spheres of ever-expanding realization. As he crosses threshold after threshold, conquering dragon after dragon, the stature of the divinity that he summons to his highest wish increases, until it subsumes the cosmos. Finally, the mind breaks the bounding sphere of the cosmos to a realization transcending all experiences of form—all symbolizations, all divinities: a realization of the ineluctable void."

Whatever the journey, it is one that ultimately leads us back home. My path has been characterized by the gifts that I needed to uncover and claim. Burlesque brought me home to myself and to my heart. If I step back and take in all the events and chain reactions in my life, a pattern begins to emerge. I can see how all the curveballs and challenges that were in my path ultimately were there so I could get back to a deeper sense of belonging to myself and residing within that authority.

Burlesque is fabulous, amazing and gorgeous, but even within its embrace, I know I am more than what I love to do.

As a fan of soul journeys and the human process, I came across the following passage which refers to Campbell's work cited above. Although life may appear to be linear as we view it, in retrospect (i.e one event follows another one and creates the conditions for the next event, etc.), it is anything but. The constant inside/out nature of my experiences are beautifully captured by this quote from Christopher Vogler in *The Writer's Journey*:

> *"I believe that much of the journey is the same for all humans, since we share many realities of birth, growth, and decay, but clearly, being a woman imposes distinct cycles, rhythms, pressures, and needs. There may be a real difference in the form of men's and women's journeys. Men's journeys may be in some sense more linear, proceeding from one outward goal to the next, while women's journeys may spin or spiral inward and outward. The spiral may be a more accurate analogue for the woman's journey than a straight line or a simple circle. Another possible model might be a series of concentric rings, with the woman making a journey towards the center and then expanding out again. The masculine need to go out and overcome obstacles, to achieve, conquer, and possess, may be replaced in the woman's journey by the drives to preserve the family and the species, make a home, grapple with emotions, come to accord, or cultivate beauty."*

I only know my own journey as a woman, and I honor the multiplicity of life experience that you bring as you read these words. I honor that life is not linear and that the universe has a crazy and wonderful way of bringing us right to where we need to be in order to learn and grow in our own way. No matter your gender or identity, your journey matters just as much to you as mine does to me.

You don't need any of the conditions that I drew into my life, but you do need to trust that deep down inside of you, there is a fire waiting to be lit and fed so that your soul can dance its truth free from restriction, oppression, and judgment.

This is your time.

Are you ready to say yes?

It is no mistake that you are reading these words right now. I firmly believe in the perfect timing of life and all the events therein. I feel that we have chosen the bodies we have at this time with all of their stories and histories and possibilities for a reason.

There are no miscalculations on why you are in your particular body with the family you have along with all the conditions that are present in your life. Life's purpose is to reveal us to us, lessons and opportunities to love and all. As we step into an increasingly uncertain future, what if we made a new commitment to anchor ourselves deeply in our hearts and moved forward from a place of joy deep within us, sparked by our free self-expression? What if we called upon the energy of love, of true union with what makes our hearts sing with delight and allow it into every corner of our lives? What shockwaves of fresh possibility could that create?

The world as we know it is changing rapidly. The old, established systems of power and control are being shaken to their core by the increased visibility of shadowy practices and the brilliant light of love and equality throwing them into stark contrast. Division is acutely inflaming our interconnections and our collective sense of identity and self.

What if we operated from a deep place of love within our hearts and consciously chose our own unique paths to fulfillment without denigrating others' experiences or pressing our will upon another?

When we show up for our own evolution with compassion, persistence and the belief that every obstacle is a possibility for growth, our lives can be better no matter what is present in our experience, we create a nexus of energy that can profoundly impact our lives, the lives of those around us, and our world as a whole.

My story is not the same as yours, but perhaps you noticed some similarities. Maybe you have seen a glimmer of your own reflection as I held up the mirror of my life. I hope that my story illuminates your own with a deeper sense of self-love and purpose for your own path.

Whether or not you have an intention to ever set foot on stage, we all have our testing grounds, our own personal stage of life. Maybe you are a rocket scientist or a mathematician. Maybe you're a kindergarten teacher, or a farmer or someone working a 9-5 job to make ends meet. No matter what you do or who you are, the proverbial stage that you step onto is yours and yours alone.

What is your truth, your creativity? What is your own sense of self-expression inspiring you to do and say? How do you want to be seen? I lovingly dare you to throw on some metaphorical (or literal) glitter and give it a go. There's no knowing until you finally try it out.

Everything in life is practice. Every opportunity to engage and connect with others over the course of our days holds a chance for us to play and get comfortable with new choices and new commitments that are grounded in deep, unapologetic self-love. Not only can our lives become vibrant with purpose and deep self-belonging, we can also have a powerful impact on our families, communities, and world by intentionally stepping into love.

Let us come home to ourselves and our hearts with the thought that we are each unique beings on our own individual soul journey. No two journeys will look alike, but each and every one is valid. Each one is replete with profound gifts to be experienced and shared along the way. Bring together everyone with their individual gifts and journeys and a vast, multi-layered, indescribable richness of experience and wisdom will emerge. We are not separate from each other. We are not separate from ourselves. We are not our bodies. We are not alone. We never have been. We can now choose to come home to our own gifts and claim them, knowing that by doing so we are contributing to a collective good that is much bigger than our individual selves. By affirming our connection to one another, we create a resonance of deep unity within ourselves that will profoundly change our world for the better.

May we all foster the courage to show up with love for ourselves and for life as we expand what we know into what is possible. May you choose to be your own ally.

May you shake what your mama gave you.

May you find your joy and own it, receive it and allow it in.

Each and every one of us has power. May we choose to use it for good and have great fun doing it. When you choose to walk with love, you might just land in your greatest joy.

Glitter is optional, but your participation isn't.

I dare you to say yes to what's in your heart. I lovingly challenge you to go after what your heart dares to dream. There's no time like the present, and I invite you to begin now.

Epilogue: I Am Still Learning

I am not done learning. I won't ever be. Becoming a better, more informed, conscious and compassionate person is a lifelong journey. It is not always an easy or comfortable journey. But it's also thrilling. Wouldn't it be easy and wonderful to know everything? Actually no, it wouldn't. Sure it's lovely to have an easy time of things, but how can we learn otherwise? I'll always remember the wonderful words of Tony Lo Mastro, one of my rebirthing teachers, when he said: "it's not comfortable and that's okay."

I value and love my teachers. Many of them I know personally. And some I don't. For the teachers I have been fortunate to have found thus far, I am grateful to the point of tears. I've shared some of their words with you in these pages. Their compassion, wisdom, and searing honesty (in some cases) have made me the person who is typing these words. Many of them impacted me not just by their learned wisdom, but what it took for them to get there.

As I write this book, I am haunted by the thought of "what if I screw up with any of this information? Will I be called out? Will I be shamed? Will someone mount a vigorous and ruinous social media campaign against me simply because of what I share and care about?" I guess I'll find out, but I am soothed by the many women, men and gender-fluid folks who fearlessly share what lies within their hearts. It is thanks to their example that I gather the courage to commit these words to paper and screen.

We are living in a time of unprecedented change.

The earth is shaking, burning, and flooding. Big companies are doing their best to distract us from the reality that is creeping and seeping into every corner of our consciousness for fear of losing profit.

I don't know what the earth will be like in 5, 10, 15 years from now, but what I do know is that the things we have taken for granted—clean air, water, food, and soil—are being threatened and harmed with a disturbing frequency. This process of awakening isn't easy or comfortable, and that's okay--as Tony would say.

I deeply believe that we have chosen these bodies and these lives on a soul level so that we may be present for the changes happening on our planet now. For the perfect learning of my own soul curriculum, I chose a white, slender body imbued and gifted with immense privilege. I am still learning according to this vessel of mine, and I am far from done.

I have felt blessed and burdened by these gifts because in many ways they hid me from the harsher realities of the world. Sure, I saw and experienced what I needed to, but my eyes are consistently opened to horrific, inhumane, heartless treatment of humans and our planet that I have not been touched by. In writing this book, I strove to tell my story and add in what I feel passionate about. I wonder, if and when the second edition of this book comes out, what I might say then.

I am acutely aware of the immaculate imperfections we all hold within our bodies and lived experiences. I believe these imperfections become fractal in their complexity when we all come into contact with one another.

I grapple with the question of how do I preach love when I feel such fury towards the groups whose beliefs run counter to my own? I wrestle with my mission and message of love in the face of hatred, violence, and the justification of anger in the form of prejudiced treatment of others.

Deep down I know that anger cannot be justified. We cannot engage in behaviors or orations that justify our fury and feelings of injustice and simultaneously create good in this world.

Yes, we can air out our feelings, but as we do so we must be responsible for what the expression of those feelings brings into being. What do we contribute by flagellating those around us with our rage? We accomplish nothing by doing so apart from achieving a momentary state of catharsis. I don't know anyone who vents and rages online only to say, "ah, I feel better now." That anger behaves like a vortex that feeds upon itself. I have to watch myself like a hawk when I get into that space, and the vigilance with which I proceed is crucial if I am to temper my message with love.

The truth is that I am saddened by how we treat each other, and the many conundrums we currently find ourselves in. My rage and grief won't do anything to contribute to the progress I desperately want to see on all levels of our lives, and so I must turn to love.

I think of the conservative Christians who rail against basic human rights and everything I hold dear as sinful and worthy of punishment. I also remember that I happen to care deeply for some conservative Christians and do not wish to hurt them. I think too of my liberal, non-religious friends whose rage at the injustices in our world push them deeper into fights that I'm not sure can be won with anger and vitriol alone. And yet, I want to hold them and their hearts lovingly in my own as I write these words.

If I want to activate the energies of change, I need to go in with love. I need to have hard conversations. I want to go in with an open heart and healthy boundaries, knowing that love is possible. It doesn't mean that a miracle will happen, but then again it just might.

For those who don't know, I'm married to a woman. I spent my young adult life being absolutely boy crazy and so it came as a surprise to everyone I knew, and especially me, when I fell in love with a short, loud, hilarious woman. Everything changed when we fell in love, and I felt hugely lucky to be welcomed into the amazing queer community of New York City.

It also opened my eyes to the fact that not everyone on the street is friendly. I was used to walking down the street and being favorably treated despite the occasional wolf whistles or leering looks. Holding my wife's hand as we walked down the streets of Brooklyn was a rude awakening. We received long, judgmental looks, and gross, occasionally super-inappropriate comments. We were also generally left alone, which is one of the gifts of living in New York. I think of the sadness I feel when someone looks at us with judgment or hate in their eyes. If I reacted the same way toward their judgment, how would that change anything at all? It would serve to grind the resistance, the hate, and the judgment even deeper into the proverbial rug we all share and are trying to clean.

When we got married in the summer of 2016, the Trump presidency was an ominous but (to our white eyes and sensibilities) impossible possibility. Our wedding vows included an acknowledgment of our ancestors who had undergone extreme persecution, loss, and crisis that brought them to America. Our wedding on the Hudson River felt like a dream come true where we could affirm our love for one another without fear or concern that our right to be married could be taken away. I acknowledge our blessed privilege to have had this experience, and I pray that all may know and experience such freedom to enter into a legal union with the person they love, whoever they may be.

The exceptional writer and activist, Sonya Renée Taylor, has had an incredible impact on me. If you don't know her, please go read her books and follow her on social media. She has educated me in the ways of whiteness that in many ways have brought our world to where it is right now. The thought that white people only do good (they/we don't) and are somehow superior (they/we aren't) are beliefs that are leading us straight to ruin. Paired with the immense wealth that the global elite hold, the upper echelons of society have neatly sequestered themselves away from any challenging or difficult conversations with layers of security and anonymity. This convenient separation is something that is practiced throughout modern society. Turning our backs or walking past injustice of any form because we don't have time, we're scared, etc. does nothing but perpetuate the problem.

Even as I write these words, I am acutely aware of how I forget about love as I attempt to assess and understand the ills of our world. I would love to step into the mind of Buddha, Jesus, Gandhi, Martin Luther King Jr., and every other leader who led fearlessly and very humanely with their heart. Here I am, writing a book about the art of the striptease and the divine presence of love. What if people laugh at me? What if they come after me? What if I commit egregious errors on these pages that become fodder for those who wish me ill?

The deeper truth is that love is everywhere. As I re-read these words, I realize much of what I have posited in these previous chapters is as much for me as it is for you. This is my first book, my first venture into the great unknown. There are zero guarantees of what lies beyond the publication of this book. Of course I'm quaking in my boots—I've never done anything like this before! I have laid my heart out on these pages and instead of dwelling in their imperfection and catastrophizing how it might be received, I choose to leave this book as an offering on the altar of the here and now. If you've read this far, I imagine you may have enjoyed what I have written because otherwise why finish the book?

I'm doing what I can with what I have. I'm figuring this out as I go along, and I find that the kinder I am to myself, the easier the lessons get. I hope that you are willing to do the same.

Acknowledgments and Gratitudes

I want to begin by thanking my parents, Sally and Paul for bringing me into this world. As your firstborn and as a girl who knew what she wanted, I thank you for your patience, support, and love. I love you both very much. And to my stepmom Kat too—thank you for your love, and support. I love you.

To Rebekkah Kronlage and Arti Roots Ross—thank you for introducing me to the sacred work of healing. Your words, guidance, and presence are always with me. Thank you for being the healing mother figures I never knew I needed.

To Emilie Conrad—thank you for being such a punk rock badass who birthed the gift of Continuum Movement. I am so grateful for your hard work and now-departed presence on this planet. Pranams to Pati Stillwater for her selfless help and work that I so richly benefitted from.

To Ron Baker—I am humbled by the embarrassment of riches you have bestowed upon me. I consider it one of the highest privileges of my life to know you, to work with you, and to learn from you. I love you so much, and am so wildly, profoundly grateful to you.

To Sondra Ray—I bow to your incredible, visionary work that helped shape my awareness and work. Thank you for being a conduit of Babaji's presence and timeless wisdom and love. Your wonderful spirit and ability to get right down into the core of any matter is a gift to us all. I am grateful to you and Markus for the sacred roles you have played in my life.

To Maureen Malone & Tony LoMastro—I love you two so much. Thank you for your selfless service and dedication to educating us about the gifts of rebirthing breathwork. I love and celebrate your hard work and the consistent outpouring of tools and love for us all to benefit from and heal our own lives.

To Michelle Locke—thank you for Wu Tao Dance, thank you for your friendship and mentorship, and thank you for being part of my soul family for many lifetimes. I love you and let's dance!

To Jennifer Urezzio—one of my favorite Scorpios ever. Thank you for your wisdom, guidance, and first pass at editing this behemoth of a book. Your no-nonsense approach to everything is wonderfully refreshing and your gift of Soul Language is priceless. I adore and love you.

To my ENORMOUS burlesque family—you crazy, gorgeous, brilliant weirdos. I love you all so much. Thank you for being my tribe and for reflecting back to me everything I love, celebrate and need to work on. From the highs to the lows and back again, I love you forever. Please keep revealing your bodies and your magic so the girls, boys, trans babies and all dancers of tomorrow and beyond can be all the richer for it.

Additional thanks, high fives and hugs to Nesreen Mahmoud and Stephanie Stanton for their excellence in coaching and for showing me that I am so much more than what I think I am. From the bottom of my heart, thank you.

To my wife, Lola, for her unending support, love, and celebration of everything I am, we are, and what we have been so massively, richly blessed with. Thank you for showing me what love looks like on the regular. I love you, woman.

About the Author

Anna Brooke is an interdisciplinary healing arts practitioner, purveyor of mirth and a lifelong dancer. Her burlesque persona, Rev. Legs Malone, has been onstage since 2006 and continues to perform, produce shows and teach burlesque both nationally and internationally. She lives in The Berkshires of Western Massachusetts with her rockstar wife Lola and their three amazing animals, Princess Pickle Pants, Jane Doe, and Helen Yeller. This is her first book.

CPSIA information can be obtained
at www.ICGtesting.com
Printed in the USA
LVHW010348110720
660357LV00002B/164

9 781733 419765